150+ Fun Things To Do In Retirement

Creative Bucket List Items For A Vibrant Life After Work (On a Budget!)
(+ Tips To Find Fun Things To Do In Your City)

By

Garrett Monroe

Contents

Contents

The Next (& Most Fun!) Chapter of Your Life

"Retirement is wonderful. It's doing nothing without worrying about getting caught at it."

-Gene Perrett, comedy writer and producer

Comedian Gene Perrett was known for his tongue-in-cheek comments, but he was on to something when he summarized retired living in the quote above.

"'Nothing?'" you may be thinking. "Why is a book about things to do in retirement recommending…nothing?"

Hold on now—we're getting there. Having rewarding activities and the financial means to pursue them is a fantastic recipe for a happy, post-employment existence. But what's retirement *really* all about? Vacations and long mornings on the golf course? Cheaper movie tickets and the opportunity to join a book club? Sure—if those things float your boat, you'll have ample time for them now. But retirement is about more than just living a life of leisure.

It's about freedom! It's about waking up each morning feeling secure in the knowledge that *you* are the one deciding what you get to do with your time. And sometimes, that something will be nothing at all.

Other times, however, it won't be. This book is designed to provide advice on all aspects of retired life. We'll look at the financial realities of preparing for a retirement that allows you to pursue your interests. We'll reflect on all the activities that retired people often enjoy. And we'll even explore the psychological factors that drive people's decisions as they get older.

We'll also acknowledge a hard truth—that not everyone finds the happiness they were hoping for in retirement. Some of us struggle with the transition of leaving a world where they had a clearly defined purpose and entering one that requires, as Perrett described, nothing from them at all.

To that end, it's worth acknowledging that you're now entering a phase of life for which you haven't been prepared. Life, until this point, has molded you into an employee. From the moment your mother led you into your preschool classroom, you were being primed for and plied with job-readiness skills.

Granted, that might be hard for some people to believe—unless they made their way into this life as a natural born "color and shape identifier"(which is nice work if you can get it). But the reality is that our school system is designed to funnel us naturally into the world of employment—a world that doesn't appropriately prepare us for a proper transition *out* of it.

And so this book's thesis is simple: Retired people are forced to create their own meaning—all on their own—for the first time in their lives. It's absolutely doable, but sometimes a little help is required along the way.

That may sound like a tall order, and it is—but we sleep easy knowing that the burden of responsibility will, in the end, fall upon you, dear reader. We can't define post-retirement bliss for you—bliss is far too subjective for that. But we can (and will) connect you with the tools you'll need to find success along the way.

And we'll have fun doing it, too. However, the advice that'll ultimately drive this book's value is thoroughly researched and evidence-supported. There's even a citation page to prove it.

But first, you might be asking yourself, "Who is this Garrett Monroe, and what does he possibly know about having fun in retirement?"

Fair question—you don't want to trust your life after years of the grind with just anyone!

The truth is that Garrett Monroe isn't just one person; it's actually a pen name for a *team* of writers with experience in retirement planning, finance, and more—and we've had a wide range of adventures between us. Some of us have also retired from our long-term careers and know all about what it's like to be on the other side of retirement—as well as all the challenges and fun that come along with it!

The entire team has a passion for connecting people with resources that'll help them live fulfilling, post-employment lives. And in this book, though we'll touch on the financials of retirement a bit, the main goal here is to help you think beyond the dollar signs and focus on what will *actually* make you happy in your sunset years.

You'll receive plenty of actionable advice that can be interpreted flexibly and as you see fit. What you'll find in the pages to follow isn't a precise map but rather an outline of possibilities. Let's get into a list of the nuggets of wisdom you'll find in this book that'll prepare you for years of retirement relaxation and revelry. **We'll tuck into:**

- How to kick your retirement blues to the curb with hobbies that enrich your life and expand your mind. Whitewater rafting for the adventurous? Book clubs for the homebodies? The possibilities are endless.

- Fun and accessible ways to stay healthy doing exercises you *actually* enjoy.

- Tips for reigniting your social life—and, if you're single, maybe even finding a special someone to travel the world with.

- Advice on how to have fun regardless of your budget. Sometimes the old clichés are true: Many of the best things in life *are* free.

So without further ado (because essentially, you've waited your whole life to peel back the pages of a guidebook on retirement, so why prolong things?), let's get started.

Chapter 1

Crafting Your Ideal Post-Work Life

"Often when you think you're at the end of something, you're at the beginning of something else."

-Fred Rogers, children's TV host and author

Retirement can feel like you're coming full circle. It's an experience that people wait their entire careers for, and yet when it comes, they don't always know what to do with themselves. The "post-career blues" are very common; in fact, rates of depression increase by about 30% within the first few years of retirement.

The psychology behind this phenomenon is well-established and represents a combination of factors. Feelings of depression tend to increase with aging, as those now out of the workforce can suddenly feel their worlds shrinking around them.

It's not hard to understand why—you're leaving a place where your role was well-defined and appreciated, and suddenly entering a realm in which you don't even have to change out of your pajamas if the mood doesn't strike you!

The transitional aspects of retirement can also extend into your finances, your community standing, your access to social interactions, and many other areas. It's a big change that you're expected to take advantage of and appreciate, but for many, making that happen is harder than they anticipated.

And that's okay.

Retirement shouldn't be a source of pressure (you experienced enough of that during the daily grind!). It should be leisure—something you enjoy. Having a list of goals, hobbies, and other interests can enrich your life. However, there's nothing wrong with spending a little time decompressing before you look for your next adventure. And sometimes, decompressing is exactly what you *should* be doing at the beginning of this new chapter.

Framing Your Retirement Mindset

It takes the average person about ten weeks to form a new habit [1]. While the word "habit" leads many people to think about dietary choices, exercise regimens, or even some odd quirks, it has a broader definition in the context of human health. The term is defined as "an action that you take automatically." You can think of a habit as your brain's autopilot setting—you don't need to think much when you're entrenched in a routine.

But when you stop working, you lose a routine that's become second nature to you, and it takes time for your brain to adjust to its new circumstances.

Some people may feel very comfortable walking out of work one day and heading off to the airport with their passports in hand the next, while others benefit from (or even require) a transitional period. If you feel like you need time to adapt to a retirement mindset, there's certainly no shame in that. Take things as slowly as you'd like without any feelings of guilt. After all, this is *your* time—and you've earned it!

Your Retirement Style: High Octane, Homebody, or Both?

Retirement allows you to explore your old hobbies in greater depth but it's also a unique opportunity to try new things as well. You may have gone through most of your adult life as a homebody, but—assuming your finances can accommodate it—you may also now have an unprecedented opportunity for travel.

Or, then again, you might not want to travel. The stereotypical notion of post-employment life is that the world opens up to you the moment you quit your job. However, even people with well-funded retirement accounts often find that they're more comfortable at home.

Studies show that the pleasure derived from travel actually tends to diminish with age. Part of this paradox is practical [2]; while mobility issues aren't always a major concern for people in their sixties, general health problems do compound with age.

But a European study published in January of 2024 revealed that only 40% of the surveyed study participants mentioned their health as the reason they choose not to travel. While there were a variety of other reasons listed, the second-most common, behind health, was a lack of interest.

It turns out that, for many, if you didn't like traveling when you were younger, there's a good chance that you still won't care for it by the time you reach retirement age. And with all the streaming options available now, who could blame you for staying home?

Jokes aside, it's a fact that the high-octane retirement stereotype isn't a natural fit for everyone.

You certainly don't need to feel pressure to live out someone else's retirement fantasy. You need to focus on the things that make *you* happy. You can absolutely consider experimenting with new things if you feel so inclined—after all, it's often said that life begins outside your comfort zone—but approach your choices with a perspective of mindfulness.

And if you do want to splurge on an experience? That's great, too! Just bear in mind that large (or excessive) post-retirement spending *does* need to be approached strategically. We'll examine the financial realities of retirement later on in the book.

However, assuming that you have the means to indulge in the occasional splurge, it's important to do so conscientiously.

Aside from travel (but also including it), many retired people report that the experiences that bring them the most joy involve human contact. Remember that your social circle may narrow considerably once you stop interacting regularly with coworkers. Large family dinners, group vacations, and even fishing/golf/hiking outings with close friends are all great ways to spend your hard-earned money and newly acquired freedom during retirement. Just keep in mind that "splurge" is a flexible term—there's no need to spend extravagantly just because you "can." In fact, many of retired life's greatest pleasures are free (or very affordable).

Crafting Your Personalized Retirement Bucket List

Once you've detoxed from the pressure of having to have a big, glamorous retirement, it's easier to focus on pursuing activities that'll actually make you happy. Some of those activities may involve calling a travel agent, while others could involve simpler hobbies or even quiet reflection.

In this section, we'll look at some ways in which you can craft a personalized retirement bucket list.

Self-Reflect: Your Likes, Dislikes, Regrets & Personality

Reaching retirement age presents many people with a paradox. On the one hand, they have much more time than they've since they started kindergarten 50 or 60-odd years earlier. On the other, the stopwatch for their time on this earth is gradually ticking.

There's a reason that we call these "the sunset years." But while retirement represents the final stage of your life, it doesn't mean that it'll necessarily be a *short* stage. After retirement, many people can expect another 20 or even 30 years. It does, however, mean that your mortality tends to weigh more heavily on the mind than it did when you were busy with work and raising a family.

Some people find the extra opportunities for reflection uncomfortable, and that's valid. However, if you push through it, that discomfort can actually be clarifying. Time is limited for all of us, and you're now in the unique position of getting to spend the rest of yours in any way you choose.

So then—what *do* you want? That should be the question that helps shape your bucket list. Think about the things you enjoy—and *also* the things you want to avoid. Consider your regrets. Are there any mistakes from your past that you can work on now that you have more time?

One very helpful way to develop a retirement itinerary is to think about how you spend your time now. Most people work for 40 to 50 hours a week. Are your retirement plans developed enough to fill even half of that time?

Interests and hobbies are great, but you may also want to start thinking about volunteer opportunities. Many people connect with charities they feel strongly about during their retirement years, and it's a fabulous way to give back to the communities they'd like to support.

Once you've inventoried your feelings and desires, you can then move on to practical considerations. Where will you find the opportunities that you're interested in? What are your financial limitations? Below, we'll look at some considerations that can further shape and refine your retirement to-do list.

Digging Into Your Roots: How Family History Shapes Your Bucket List

Family history is inescapable. It's coursing through your veins right now—even at this age—still shaping your health, your feelings, and your future. This doesn't necessarily mean that you're ensnared by your roots, but it *does* mean that your family has influenced your life considerably up until this point and will continue to do so throughout your retirement.

What does that mean in the context of making plans? Well, it doesn't have to mean anything, but some people find it helpful to think about what their parents were like when *they* reached retirement age. Were they healthy? What physical or emotional hardships did they need to navigate?

To be clear, you're not doomed to repeat the circumstances of the past. Improvements in medicine are happening every day, and retired people are healthier than ever before. Still, knowing your family history can inform your expectations and shape your behavior.

If, for example, you have a long family history of congestive heart failure, you may decide to be extra mindful of cardiovascular health as you age. If several generations of relatives suffered from arthritis, you may decide to make a point of exploring physically demanding activities now while you still feel healthy enough to enjoy them.

Money Matters: Curating a Bucket List Within Your Budget

Hopefully, you've already laid the initial groundwork for your retirement. A study recently found that many people begin saving for retirement as early as the age of 22 [3]. However, true "nest-egg" building doesn't usually begin in earnest until most people are in their thirties. It's usually then that the average person has established themselves professionally and taken care of several other key milestones, like saving for a house and a car.

There's a lot of doom and gloom around the topic of retirement savings. You'll hear people say things like, "You can never save enough money for retirement!" Obviously, that's not true because thousands of people worldwide retire every day, and most of them aren't Warren Buffet!

So what *is* true? How much money do you actually need to have before you can safely retire? Well, the answer may surprise you. It isn't the lofty figure of one million dollars that financial advisors have historically recommended. In fact, it's not necessarily a set number at all.

What matters most is that you have a sustainable debt-to-income ratio throughout retirement. Ideally, you'll have paid off all of your major loans and obligations by the time you exit the workforce. This means that you aren't worrying about car or house payments anymore, but it also means that you (hopefully) are no longer financially responsible for any dependents.

Assuming that you're debt-free (or close to it) and receiving enough income through social security, your 401(k), or pension plan, you should at the very least be able to retire without needing to worry about food and shelter.

Of course, you also need to make sure that your healthcare needs are being met. Medicare typically kicks in when you turn 65, which is why this has historically been a popular age for retirement. It's also generally true that most people are healthy enough at 65 to comfortably pursue their version of post-retirement bliss.

Let's say that you do have your post-retirement income—you've managed your debts responsibly and figured out how you'll handle your healthcare. What other considerations do you need to address before you can start working on your post-retirement bucket list?

Ultimately, that'll depend on what you hope to accomplish. The younger you start working on your retirement plans, the easier it'll be to finance big-ticket things like world travel. If you started making contributions to a Roth IRA account at age 35 (continuing with the annual maximum contribution of $6,500 at the time of writing), your account could easily be valued in the high six figures at the time of your retirement.

Financial advisors refer to the period between your mid-thirties to your mid-fifties as the accumulation phase of your retirement planning. It's during this time that you can be the most ambitious in terms of how aggressively you invest—and how big you dream.

At this stage, you're not only putting away money that'll benefit the most from compound interest—you're also making life choices that have a major impact on your long-term finances. Do you buy a big house that'll limit your ability to make retirement contributions? Or do you spend more conservatively with the hope of boosting your long-term savings potential?

Circumstances don't always favor financial prudence. Most people experience years during which they can't maximize their 401(k) contributions or boost their independent investment portfolio. And that's okay. When you hit your fifties, the considerations begin to shift a little bit.

Currently, you most likely have a pretty decent idea of what your access to post-retirement capital will look like. You'll know your account balances and have a pretty clear understanding of at what age you'll be able to afford to live without employment.

At this stage, most people are focused on eliminating any residual debts and making a final push on their retirement savings. So while fortune tends to favor those who plan early, there are many opportunities along the way to create conditions for a retirement that'll make you happy.

Plan Realistically

What's the takeaway from all this? Simply out, you don't have to be rich to have a happy retirement. Forward thinking from a young age can help you achieve your retirement goals, but almost anyone can enjoy their sunset years if they make wise choices.

That said, don't make Champagne plans on a beer budget. There are pleasures to be had in even the simplest of circumstances. Henry David Thoreau, philosopher and lifelong advocate for simple living, had this to say on the subject:

"Most of the luxuries and many of the so-called comforts of life are not only not indispensable, but positive hindrances to the elevation of mankind."

Which is a sort of formal way of saying that we're often happier living an uncluttered life. (Or, in other words, perhaps you should add getting a library card to your retirement to-do list to finally clear out those dusty bookshelves! Hey, whatever strikes you—as long as you're living within your means.)

Embracing Your Locale: Leveraging Your Geographic Location

Learning to take advantage of local opportunities is a great and often affordable way to enjoy a fulfilling retirement. Most cities will have free or inexpensive resources that can provide you with plenty of recreational opportunities.

The quip we made earlier about how you might want to add getting a library card to your retirement to-do list? It's actually good advice. The uninitiated often assume that libraries are just about peddling books, but many of them offer a variety of classes and opportunities that can provide you with consistent social outlets during your retirement.

In some public libraries, you can find classes and activities on everything from learning another language and dance to automotive repair.

Thinking beyond books and the beautiful people who work with them, you may also find community groups where you live that focus on local history, city beautification, or other volunteer opportunities. Churches, rec centers, and other local organizations are all excellent ways to form social connections.

You don't have to limit your thinking to your own backyard, either. If you want to dip your toes into the world of travel, you might first want to think about looking for destinations within a 100-mile radius. This will allow you to save money by traveling by car instead of airplane, and it'll also be a relatively stress-free way to explore your interests. Plus, nothing beats the roadside scenery en route to your destination. You can't find that 37,000 feet above ground!

And you may even be surprised by the travel opportunities available within your region of the country. Even if you don't live within a quick driving distance of a major city, you're likely close to some fun tourist destinations that you've, for whatever reason, never been to before. Also, if these places have never appealed to you in the past, keep in mind that our tastes tend to change as we, ahem, become wiser.

Influence of Relationships: Incorporating Friends & Family Into Your Plans

Naturally, retirement affords you some great opportunities to focus on the relationships that mean the most to you. However, you can't expect your personal relationships to automatically blossom and improve the moment you stop working.

There's a reason that many retirees experience social isolation so acutely, as many of the people in your life may still be working a 9-to-5 schedule. Your life is moving at a different rhythm now, which can make it hard to synchronize with your loved ones.

More challenging yet is when deeper connections *could* be made were it not for an apparent lack of motivation or availability on the other party's side. In other words, you may find that your adult children aren't around as often as you'd like.

Sometimes, you have to meet people where they're at. Start by thinking about how you'd like your post-work relationships to go. Set reasonable expectations and communicate them with your loved ones—they may very well reciprocate your feelings. Conversely, they may communicate different desires or expectations. Either way, it'll likely take a bit of effort on your part.

Ability Is What You're Capable of Doing: Considering Your Physical Ability & Health

If you're retiring between 60 and 65 years old, you can (hopefully) expect to enjoy reasonably good health for years to come. However, it's still a good idea to think realistically about your physical limitations. If you have bad knees, you may not want to plan a three-month hiking expedition along the Appalachian Trail. If you're saddled with a heart condition, you may choose to avoid lengthy international trips in favor of quieter, lower-stress pleasures.

Always speak with your doctor to find out what they recommend. Not only will they help you to develop realistic expectations but they may also provide valuable advice on how to safely execute your retirement plans.

Unleashing Your Inner Picasso: Incorporating Your Talents & Skills

Now's a great time to revisit interests that you set to the side years ago. Maybe you've always liked painting—or at least the idea of painting. Maybe you used to be a fairly decent creative writer. Or perhaps you've always wanted to make your own cheese at home but never had the time.

Maybe you didn't even *know that* people could make their own cheese at home until you read that last sentence (and now you're quite curious about it). Talents, skills, and hobbies are great building blocks for choosing activities that excite and interest you throughout your retirement.

Bucket List Questionnaire: A Guide to Kickstart Your Journey

Below, we've compiled a list of a few prompts that'll help kickstart your retirement plans. These questions are designed to make you think about your interests, as well as the circumstances that are most relevant to your retirement. **Ask yourself the following:**

1. What social or environmental causes are you passionate about, and how would you like to contribute to them during your retirement?

2. Reflecting on your current relationships, which ones would you like to deepen or explore further? Are there new connections that you'd like to create?

3. What talents or hobbies have you always wanted to explore or develop further? How can you incorporate these into your retirement activities?

4. Are there new skills or concepts that you've been eager to explore? What learning opportunities or courses would you like to pursue?

5. What destinations or experiences have you always dreamt of exploring? How does travel fit into your retirement plans?

6. How do you plan to maintain or improve your physical and mental well-being? Are there specific fitness activities or wellness practices that you'd like to prioritize?

7. What's your ideal financial situation in retirement, and how do you plan to achieve and maintain it? Are there adjustments you need to make in your lifestyle or spending habits?

8. How do you envision giving back to your community? Are there local organizations you'd like to support or be actively involved in?

9. Do you see yourself working part-time or volunteering? If so, how often?

10. What experiences have brought you the most joy in the past? Are there ways you can explore those opportunities now?

If you don't have clear answers to these questions yet, that's more than okay. After all, it takes around 40 years of employment for most people to reach retirement! You don't have to know exactly what the rest of your life will look like the moment you walk out of your workplace for the last time. The beautiful thing about this stage of life is that *you* are calling the shots now, so feel free to make plans at your own pace.

And speaking of those plans, the rest of this book will give you countless options to choose from so that you can build a vibrant life after you're through with punching the time clock once and for all!

Key Takeaways

- Retirement is meant to be joyful, but it can create new stressors.

- Psychological surveys indicate that the best way to keep the post-employment blues at bay is to pursue activities you enjoy—particularly social ones.

- Having a large nest egg for your retirement is nice, but there are plenty of affordable ways to enjoy your sunset years, too.

- Your current hobbies and interests are a great place to start when thinking about ways to enrich your life. But you also shouldn't be afraid to try new things!

- Using your current schedule as a template for planning retirement activities is a fantastic way to start generating ideas.

Buyer Bonus

Want to enjoy retirement even more?! We're offering two FREE downloads that are exclusive to our book readers!

First, the **Retirement Movie Marathon PDF**. We've handpicked 20 feel-good films that are more than just flicks—they're gateways to laughter, inspiration, and heartwarming journeys. From laugh-out-loud comedies to soul-stirring romances, each movie is a toast to the joys and adventures of retirement.

Second, the **Adventure Checklist: 20 Outdoor Activities for Retirees**! This is your all-access pass to excitement, exploration, and the sheer joy of the great outdoors. Whether you're looking to reconnect with nature, pump up the adrenaline, or simply try something new and delightful, we've handpicked 20 activities to add zest to your days.

To download your bonuses, go to monroemethod.com/retirement-fun or simply scan the QR code below (just use the camera app on your smartphone!).

Chapter 2

I Feel Good: Health & Well-Being in Retirement

"It's health that is the real wealth. Not pieces of gold or silver."
-Mahatma Gandhi

The above quote is a fairly accurate insight for anyone preparing for retirement. To be fair, you've likely spent the last few decades accumulating material wealth to prepare for this stage of your life. But without optimal health, you may not be able to enjoy your time the way you hope or expect to. In this chapter, we'll take a look at some ways in which you can improve your health and well-being to enjoy the happiest retirement possible.

This will include physical fitness recommendations (everyone's favorite!), but it'll also involve tips on how to enjoy excellent mental and intellectual health as well. Many of these tips are designed to employ a holistic approach to health and wellness.

In other words, they're all about setting yourself up for success by creating natural conditions within which your body can thrive. The chemicals responsible for happiness and relaxation already exist in your brain, and these recommendations are designed to help *activate* them.

Perpetual Exploration & Other Natural Highs

Mental stimulation has many proven benefits, not only in providing people with a satisfying way to spend their time but also in improving mental acuity [4]. Many experts refer to this process colloquially as "mental workouts," or gym sessions for your brain.

Obviously, fiddling around with daily crossword puzzles doesn't exert the same sweat and toil as free weights (with the exception of the tricky Times' Sunday puzzle, perhaps), but the concept is fairly similar when it comes to exercising one of your most important organs—your brain.

When you engage in activities that stretch your mind, your brain is forced to remain active, which can effectively delay memory loss and other forms of mental decline.

The good news is that remaining mentally active doesn't have to be boring. It doesn't even have to involve pursuing activities that you aren't interested in. It might mean taking your current hobbies and finding a way to explore them in ways that are both rewarding and engaging.

For example, if you don't like crossword puzzles but you do enjoy literature, make sure that you set aside time to read every day. Reading produces more or less the same cognitive benefits as a challenging crossword puzzle, but without the constant racking of your brain (as in, *"What the *&^% is 14 Across?!?"*).

You can get these benefits from reading almost anything—a whodunit novel, a celebrity memoir, or an article in your favorite magazine. However, the benefits you experience will vary based on the complexity of the text. If you push yourself a little with books you find challenging, it'll deepen the mental reward.

Ultimately, and as with everything else, it's all about balance. If you think you can commit to reading Dickens every day, great! If you think that you'll have better luck building regular reading habits with bestselling thrillers, that's also fine. It comes down to consistency.

Here's a breakdown of what your reading/brain-teaser regimen hopes to achieve:

- **Brain Health and Cognitive Reserve:** Regular engagement in mentally stimulating activities, such as solving crosswords and reading, has been linked to the maintenance of brain health and the development of cognitive reserve. The latter term refers to the brain's ability to withstand damage and to function effectively despite age-related changes. Research suggests that mentally challenging activities contribute to building this cognitive reserve, potentially reducing the risk of cognitive decline and neurodegenerative diseases.

- **Stress Reduction and Mental Well-Being:** Engaging in activities like reading can have a positive impact on your mental health by reducing stress levels. Studies indicate that reading fiction in particular can provide an escape and relaxation, promoting mental prowess and reducing the physiological effects of stress.

- **Quality Sleep Promotion:** Establishing a routine of reading or engaging in relaxing intellectual activities before bedtime has been associated with improved sleep quality. Adequate, proper sleep is crucial for overall health, including cognitive wellness.

As long as you can commit to participating in these activities every day, you'll reap the benefits. However, sporadic mental stimulation practices are a little like going to the gym but only sitting at the smoothie bar (admittedly, we've been guilty of that in the past ourselves). Sure, you'll accumulate a few steps walking from your car into the building, but it won't be enough to see significant benefits.

Expressing Yourself Through Art

Artistic expression is also a valid and effective way of stimulating your mind [5]. This is true for participating in art projects but it can also apply to situations in which you're actively reflecting on the meaning behind a painting.

Scientists have performed brain scans on people while they're looking at art, and the findings were interesting. Not only does thinking about art heavily engage your brain, but looking at different types of paintings can potentially trigger different responses within your mind.

The next time you go to an art museum, consider making a careful exploration of several different types of galleries. It might just be the intellectual equivalent of doing a carefully planned rotation around the gym.

Just some of the benefits of pursuing art for health benefits include:

- **Emotional Expression:** Art provides a non-verbal way of expressing emotions, allowing you to convey feelings that may be challenging to articulate verbally.

- **Stress Reduction:** Engaging with art has been linked to reduced stress levels. The act of creating art, as well as immersing yourself in the visual experience of it, can promote relaxation and alleviate tension.

- **Enhanced Perspective and Reflection:** Art encourages contemplation and introspection, fostering a deeper understanding of yourself and the world. By exploring different artistic perspectives, you can gain insights and broaden your worldview.

- **Sense of Accomplishment:** Creating art—whether through drawing, painting, or other mediums—can instill a sense of achievement and boost your self-esteem. Completing an art piece provides a tangible representation of your creativity and efforts.

Keep in mind that these aren't just generalizations—artistic experiences trigger a serotonin release in your brain, making you feel physically good. The quality of the art and how much you personally enjoy it absolutely influence the extent of the benefits. However, the same study referenced earlier found that *any* type of art viewing can activate your brain in beneficial ways.

Art Doesn't Have to Be Visual

While some of the benefits described above—like using pictures to express thoughts you don't have the words for—are the exclusive domain of visual arts, other creative pursuits provide similar benefits.

31

You can also stimulate your mind and engage honestly with your emotions through creative writing. The definition of what this process entails is flexible; creative writing is simply any form of writing that's designed to be entertaining. This could mean fiction, but it could also mean sitting down to tell your life story—and we all have one of *those* to tell.

Retirement might be a particularly great time to think about writing a memoir. Don't worry if the story of your life and where you've been doesn't amount to hundreds of thousands of words—even a few dozen pages that you put out for friends and family can be a rewarding use of your time.

Studies have shown that creative writing is great for stress reduction, improved self-understanding, increased cognitive function, and even easier decision making. You don't have to embody the anguished, scotch-slinging writer stereotype (unless that's your thing!)—there are a lot of people having fun at the keyboard, just sitting down and getting their thoughts onto the page. And whether you choose to have a Glenfiddich on hand while you're doing it is up to you.

Lifelong Learner

Another great way to keep your mind active is to participate in courses and seminars about topics that you like. We mentioned in the previous chapter that libraries are great resources for connecting with free classes, but the options extend onward from there.

Some universities will also allow senior citizens to attend select classes for free or a reduced price. You won't get college credits for these courses, **but you may just learn a little more about something you**

care about and keep your mind fresh while doing it. Just a handful of academic institutions that offer these courses include:

- California State University

- Clemson University

- Colorado State University

- Georgia Institute of Technology

- Rutgers

If you're interested in taking a class that hasn't advertised a free or reduced price, contact the school about their audit policy. Classroom auditing allows you to sit in on classes without taking tests or completing homework (which, as we all know, are never the most fun parts of learning something new).

The sky really is the limit with continued learning opportunities, but feel free to think outside the box. While it's natural to consider fun and lighthearted classes like cooking, photography, art history, and so on, you may also decide to challenge yourself a little bit. Enroll in a philosophy course or two. Consider learning a second language. Study comparative literature. The deeper you stimulate your mind, the more you'll experience the mental benefits of lifelong learning. And who knows? You might even discover a new passion along the way.

Crosswords & Brain Boosters

Daily puzzles and other fun intellectual exercises are an easy way to get your regular intellectual reps in. They can be accomplished leisurely with your morning coffee and don't take up much of your time. You can even get creative and competitive with them—see if you can beat your spouse's time on the daily crossword puzzle each morning, or challenge a neighbor to a daily word duel.

Some brain teaser apps have social features that allow you to compare your scores to people living all over the world, and these are great for people who are competitively motivated. **Below are a few popular mental agility apps that are easy to use:**

- **Lumosity:** Offers a variety of games and puzzles designed by neuroscientists to improve cognitive skills such as memory, attention, flexibility, and problem solving

- **CogniFit Brain Fitness:** Offers brain training exercises backed by scientific research to help improve cognitive abilities such as memory, attention, and processing speed

- **Personal Zen:** Uses a game-based approach to reduce stress and anxiety

- **Brain Trainer Special:** Offers a collection of brain-training games and puzzles designed to improve memory, concentration, and mental agility

- **Happify:** Focuses on promoting emotional well-being and positive psychology through engaging activities and exercises

Doing Well by Doing Good

While you likely won't ever confuse pitching in at a food pantry with reading Plato, it's just as mentally valuable. Volunteering can provide important brain stimulation in the form of human interactions. Here's an important thought to keep on the backburner at all times: *How can I find ways to interact with the outside world today?*

There are no doubt countless volunteer activities on offer within your community. If there's a charity you care about, that's a no-brainer way to contribute. You could also look into animal shelters, food banks, and church group opportunities. Once you start poking around, you'll find that there's no shortage of organizations willing to accept free labor— and plus, you're done with punching the time clock anyway, remember?)

Also, as mentioned earlier, social isolation is a constant concern for retired people. Volunteering can be an excellent way to eliminate that risk and contribute to a cause that you truly care about. You'll do some great things for your community, meet some friends along the way, and improve your mental agility as well.

The Joy of Mentoring: Guiding the Next Generation

Mentoring may seem like an antiquated concept, but it's actually on the rise. Many businesses are mandating it for new hires because it has proven benefits both for the mentor and the mentee—and those benefits all go back to social interactions.

Having the opportunity to share wisdom is a rewarding and mentally stimulating experience that many retirees find enjoyable. It's also beneficial to younger people who find themselves genuinely benefitting from the essential wisdom that comes from experience.

The world changes a lot over time, but basic human experiences remain largely the same. We've all had many highs and lows during our adult lives—loss, insecurity, possibly financial hardship, and certainly difficult choices.

These are all valuable experiences, the lessons from which can benefit the next generation. When you engage in mentorship opportunities, you're truly helping other people, and they're helping you in return—even just by lending a willing and enthusiastic ear.

You don't have to be Socrates, shouting your ideas on the town square for all to hear. Simple advice and stories go a long way, and there are many organizations that work to connect adults with children or teenagers who need a little extra guidance. These arrangements can be a great way to help your community while also acquiring a new social outlet. **The following are a few mentoring-related volunteering opportunities worth considering in which you can impart your valuable wisdom:**

- **Big Brothers/Big Sisters:** This is a youth-mentoring organization designed to connect adults with children aged five years and up. The kids who enter the program are usually dealing with some sort of risk factor that could disrupt their life trajectory—and that's where you can come in.

- **YMCA Youth Mentoring:** The YMCA offers many different types of mentoring programs, from educational classes involving art and athletics to sit-down opportunities for discussions with at-risk youth.

- **Girls on the Run:** This is an athletic initiative designed to promote self-love and confidence in young women, regardless of their abilities.

- **I Could Be:** This is an online mentoring opportunity that connects adults with high school students all over the country.

While the program focuses on career readiness, it's also about fostering intergenerational connections.

Walkin' On Sunshine: Overcoming Health Challenges

Health struggles happen—and as we age, we come to know that simple truth all too well. If you're dealing with mental or physical impairments that diminish your ability to enjoy retirement, it's important to keep a positive attitude. While that sounds like the sort of frustrating advice that only a healthy person could offer, it absolutely has proven benefits.

Mindfulness activities are an amazing way to stay upbeat because they're centered around focusing on the present. And that feeling of presence is key, as anxiety and emotional discomfort are often what psychologists call "past/future orientation."

In other words, you remain upset because something bad happened to you, or you're worried about how that thing will have an ongoing impact on your life. However, if you can train your mind to focus only on the present, you may find that things aren't all that bad. Your challenge remains, but not all the worrying that went along with it.

Various studies have found that patients with a positive attitude recover from surgery or other medical procedures faster than those who don't. These observations suggest that it's all a question of mind over matter. It may also be that a positive attitude makes it easier to commit to practices more conducive to health—proper nutrition, exercise, physical therapy, and so on.

Either way, it's important to hone your outlook and ensure that it's as optimistic as possible. What's the benefit of being a sad sack, anyhow? We can't think of any, and neither should you.

There are many ways to enjoy physical activities even when you *aren't* feeling your best. For example, yoga can be endlessly modified to accommodate people of various abilities and strengths.

There are also plenty of adaptive sports—swimming, wheelchair basketball, and even "running" opportunities for people in wheelchairs.

If you currently experience physical limitations, start thinking about activities that you'd would like to engage in. Chances are there's a modification available that'll allow you to pursue them—even if it may look a little different than you expected! "Normal" can be boring anyhow.

Tried & True Health & Wellness Activities

Many "active" pursuits can seem suspiciously like leisurely, docile hobbies when taken at face value. However, these behaviors—particularly when done the right way—can produce significant health benefits.

All the activities featured below have the uniting commonality of taking place outside. Spending time in the great outdoors is linked to better mental and emotional health, as it's a holistic way to trigger a serotonin response in your brain [6].

Simply put, serotonin is a biological transmitter that regulates your mood. When serotonin levels are high, you'll generally feel relaxed and possibly even full of joy. To that end, many of the suggestions below perform double duty—not only do they keep you active but they also improve your mindset.

Golf

If you like to head out to the golf course with beer and cigars, you're likely not going to reap all the possible health benefits from this activity (but no judgment here!).

That said, even while partaking in smoking and alcohol, the experience wouldn't be a total loss. You'd still get a little bit of exercise—and even riding in a cart, most golfers log about three miles worth of steps!

That number, as you'd imagine, jumps up radically if you walk 18 holes and carry your own bag. In that case, you can walk five or six miles and burn hundreds of calories. Golf is a great way to regulate your weight and get exercise—and it doesn't demand a lot from your joints. The golf swing itself is also a minor workout that activates multiple muscle groups. Duffers delight: The more times you have to hit the ball, the fitter you'll be by the end of your round! (Just don't blame us if you bogey the whole back nine.)

Hiking

The health benefits of this activity tend to be a little more straightforward—you set out pretty much knowing that you're in for a long, solid walk. Often, this walk also involves carrying gear and navigating hills, which can further increase the health value of your pursuit.

People also pay good money for guided hikes (dressed up with the hip term "forest bathing"), which is basically just a clever way to get people to pay for something they could've done for free. The "forest bathing" concept is designed as a mindfulness activity, encouraging people to relax by paying attention to their surroundings.

What these guided hikes are actually selling is the serotonin mentioned earlier. There's no need to pay some millennial a chunk of change to walk you through the woods (though you *might* want to consider this for the more challenging hikes that can be a little dangerous). Pick your favorite trail and take note of your surroundings to get an extra little health boost for your trouble.

Also, note that there are plenty of affordable and rewarding travel destinations that await hikers. Retirement could be a great time to take a tour of our country's remarkable (though often underutilized) national park system.

Fishing

Fishing is a largely sedentary activity that won't do much to help you get your steps in. It can be folded into a larger nature experience like a hiking trip, but it also has independent health value. Casting is a low-impact workout that activates multiple muscle groups, and it's great for people who can't pound on their joints for an hour at the gym anymore. **Some excellent fishing spots in the US to consider:**

- **Florida Keys, Florida:** Known for tarpon, snapper, and grouper, along with its clear waters and proximity to photo-worthy locations like coral reefs and the Mangrove islands.

- **Kenai River, Alaska:** Salmon fishing abounds here. While your surroundings will depend on where you set up shop, the river cuts through the beautiful Alaskan wilderness. There are plenty of exciting opportunities for animal interactions along its shores.

- **Outer Banks, North Carolina:** Striped bass and tuna feature heavily in this popular spot The Outer Banks also provides breathtaking coastal views of the Atlantic ocean.

- **Lake Okeechobee, Florida:** Bass is the catch of the day in this lake. One of the largest freshwater lakes in the country, the area is surrounded by marshes and wetlands.

- **Lake Erie, Ohio/Pennsylvania/New York:** Known for walleye and bass, the waters of Lake Erie lap up against the shores of rural or forested areas, but also highly industrialized cities. Because this lake is so massive, your surroundings can change radically based on where you stay.

You'll also get the mental and emotional benefits that'll come from any nature experience. Also, bonus points if you eat what you catch. While the nutritional value of fish can vary from species to species, most are rich in Omega acids—healthy fats that can benefit your heart health.

Plus, you can take a picture with your catch of the day and brag to your fishing buddies.

Aaaaah…Spas & Hot Springs

Before you book that day trip to a therapeutic retreat, take the advertised health benefits that spas and hot springs tout with a grain of epsom salt. If you comb through many spa websites, you'll see an impressive range of promises—everything from reducing your anxiety to providing tangential disease prevention. In other words, it can't be proven that spas increase your disease immunity, but studies do show that people who use spa services regularly have lower rates of illness.

And they likely do, but not because of the unique mineral properties of hot spring water. It's simply because spa services relax you. Relaxation releases serotonin, dopamine, and other pleasing chemicals that activate your brain's stress reduction response.

Relaxation does have a strong correlation with disease prevention and even symptom alleviation [7]. Stress can produce internal inflammation, high blood pressure, an accelerated heart rate, and sleeplessness—all of which can result in further health complications.

The bottom line? A little bit of self-pampering here and there can go a long way toward improving your long-term health. There are numerous hot springs throughout the country that can be great for helping heat you up and chill you out at the same time. **We've selected a few below:**

- **Hot Springs, Arkansas:** Nestled in the Ouachita Mountains, Hot Springs offers a picturesque setting with thermal springs surrounded by lush greenery and hiking trails.

- **Strawberry Park Hot Springs, Colorado:** Situated near Steamboat Springs, Strawberry Park Hot Springs provides a rustic, natural ambiance with geothermal pools set against the backdrop of the Rocky Mountains.

- **Calistoga Hot Springs, California:** Located in the heart of Napa Valley, Calistoga Hot Springs offers a serene atmosphere with rolling vineyards, creating a relaxing environment for visitors.

- **Chena Hot Springs, Alaska:** Chena Hot Springs, near Fairbanks, is surrounded by the breathtaking Alaskan wilderness, providing a perfect backdrop for soaking in hot springs, especially during winter's phenomenal northern lights displays.

- **Pagosa Springs, Colorado:** Situated in the state's southwest, Pagosa offers hot springs surrounded by the San Juan Mountains, creating a scenic and tranquil environment for relaxation.

Wellness Travel on Any Budget

Traveling doesn't have to cost a fortune and, as shown above, wellness activities can cover a lot of ground. Whether you want to do a spa weekend or spend some time improving your health in the woods, there are most likely some affordable options available within driving distance of your home.

Online rental platforms like Airbnb make it even easier to plan affordable trips. While the sticker price of these rentals is often identical to hotel rooms, you can save in the long run by taking advantage of their kitchens to avoid pricey restaurant bills.

And remember the value of exploring the national park system— camping trips are often a free or very low-cost way to travel without breaking the bank.

Online Platforms & Tools for Health After 55

Digital technology makes it incredibly easy to access information and engage in health activities. It can be a great resource for finding brain teasers, crossword puzzles, and some of the other mentally stimulating resources described earlier.

It can also be a great way to access health and wellness tools, set and track fitness goals, and find ways to keep yourself entertained during your workout.

Fitness Trackers: Monitoring Your Health

The modern fixation with "getting your steps in" is a little contrived. The idea that you need to take 10,000 steps a day was actually part of a marketing campaign for the 1964 Olympics in Japan! The number was chosen because, in Japanese script, the way 10,000 is written looks a little like a person being physically active [8]. Leave it to the innovative Japanese to have had such a huge influence on our fitness goals all these years later.

So the idea that 10,000 steps is some kind of a golden number is fiction, but it's not entirely valueless. Scientists have found a correlative relationship between hitting your step count and a wide range of health benefits.

This includes everything from improving your cardiovascular health to reducing the risk of dementia by as much as 50%. It's not exactly clear why, although researchers think it may be a secondary benefit from other outcomes of being active. Walking reduces stress levels and improves your cardiovascular health. Both are qualities that can reduce your risk of degenerative memory loss.

Fitness trackers like Fitbit, Garmin, or Apple Watch make it easy to set goals and evaluate a wide range of health metrics. Today's fitness trackers can even keep an eye on your heart rate and blood pressure, which can be very helpful in boosting your heart health and detecting health problems before they escalate.

But if you don't want to splurge on an expensive fitness tracker, you don't have to. Most smartphones have a health app that can track your steps as long as you've got your phone on you (they may be a tad less accurate than the fitness trackers, but still altogether helpful).

Mental Health Apps

These efficient apps can provide you with tips on how to take care of your emotional health, learn more about psychological concepts, and even connect almost immediately with mental health support.

Not only do these apps tear down physical barriers to support, but many people find them more comfortable than sitting across from a stranger and spilling their guts. If you take mental health seriously but aren't sure if regular therapeutic support is right for you, mental health apps could be an excellent way to get support that stays within your comfort zone.

Below are some popular mental health apps that you might want to check out:

- **Calm:** This app provides guided meditation and sleep-assistance content designed to facilitate rest and wellness.

- **Headspace:** A particularly dreamy option, Headspace specializes in "sleepcasts"—podcasts that you can play as you lay down for bed. They generally encourage you to think about calming environments and other soothing things designed to facilitate rest.

- **Happify:** Facilitating positive thinking through games, Happify has users fill out a quick survey when they make their account, who are then connected with content that fits their unique needs.

- **Talkspace Counseling:** Talkspace provides users with video or text-based therapy, allowing you to connect with mental health professionals remotely. It's compatible with many insurance plans, making most sessions affordable.

- **BetterHelp:** Similar to Talkspace, but it allows a little more flexibility. You can choose your therapist based on your preferred criteria, and you have a wider range of services to peruse (such as couples counseling).

Brain Training, Health Coaching & Music Apps

Then there's the miscellaneous section of the wellness app spectrum. Here we're referring to everything from brain-training apps that provide daily mental stimulation, to health coaching applications that may provide you with tailored health modules or even connect you with a remote fitness professional.

While you're planning out your retirement fitness routine, don't forget to stock up on some of the many digital entertainment resources out there. **Look into some popular music apps like:**

- Spotify

- Apple Music

- Amazon Music Unlimited

- iHeartRadio

- YouTube Music

These are great ways to find music that you enjoy working out to. You can also find interesting podcasts that provide entertainment, and potentially even offer health and wellness tips.

There's a wide world of digital entertainment and support resources available. Not only do these tools help you make informed health and wellness choices but they're also often free or affordable, making them a great way to stretch your retirement dollars while taking good care of yourself.

Key Takeaways

- Keeping your mind active can help reduce the "retirement blues."

- It can also strengthen your mental acuity in much the same way that working out builds muscle strength.

- Activities like reading and writing can provide a fun way to keep your mind occupied.

- Don't neglect your emotional health either! Mental health apps are a great way to take care of yourself while staying within your comfort zone—and you can also find some fantastic new tunes along the way.

Chapter 3

We Are the Champions: Physical Activities for Every Fitness Level

"The pain you feel today will be the strength you feel tomorrow."
-Stephen Richards, self-help author and motivational speaker

Richards hit the nail on the head with this quote. Fitness is tricky—the pain is immediate (we don't like that) and the rewards are almost always far off in the future (we also don't like *that*).

However, when you push through the pain and develop consistent habits, you'll begin to see lasting results sooner than you might think.

In this chapter, we'll further build upon some of the fitness ideas examined in Chapter Two, and we'll look at fun ways to move your body no matter your limitations.

Daily Movement Ideas for Different Fitness Levels

All the ideas presented in this section are designed to get you moving while pursuing activities that you enjoy. The common themes are motion and consistency—if you can keep yourself moving on a daily basis, it'll have an eventual and lasting impact on your health. Makes sense, yes?

However, many people make the mistake of selecting workout routines that are physically beneficial but not emotionally enjoyable. These regimens aren't always a good idea because they often, as you'd guess, result in not keeping up with them. You quit because you aren't having fun.

So let's explore some recommendations below, as we think that they're sustainable ways to enjoy fitness in your retirement years.

Gardening: Blooming with Plants

It's perhaps forgivable for someone who's never gardened before to underestimate its physical challenges and rewards. After all, how helpful can it really be to stare at a bunch of pansies? But the truth may surprise you.

Some gardening activities can be extremely strenuous, like digging up a new bed or even hauling soil, fertilizer, and mulch. Other activities, like picking weeds, positioning new plants, and performing your daily watering, are less demanding. However, they all get you moving outside.

Gardening is also strongly associated with a wide range of mental and emotional benefits. The old recommendation of "stopping to smell the flowers" is actually rooted in science. Scents like lemon, lavender, and other fragrant plants have been shown to alter blood chemistry in a way that reduces anxiety. The study, first performed on rats in Japan, has been scaled to humans. (We should also note that while the essential oil boom has drifted into extreme and often not scientifically supported directions, it *is* evidence-based [13]).

Smelling flowers is one of the easiest—and most pleasant—ways to regulate your mood. Dig that garden for your heart, and then sit in it with a mug of tea for your brain.

Walk This Way: Local Parks, Dog Walking & Hiking Clubs

Taking a walk in the park is a great way to enjoy nature, get out of your house, and experience the mental and emotional benefits of spending time outside. You can double down on these benefits by joining a walking club (there's a pretty good chance that your community will have multiple options to choose from) or walking a dog (the pooch parents in your neighborhood will love you for it).

Walking or hiking clubs have the additional bonus of facilitating social interactions, and dog walking can trigger a similar response in your brain. Emotional support animals have grown in popularity because they're a scientifically supported way to reduce stress.

Cortisol is your body's stress hormone. It's there to trigger a flight or fight response in emergency situations. While it has an obvious value during crisis scenarios, it's often triggered by non-emergency events.

When you feel bad because you're worried about making a deadline at work, for example, you're experiencing the negative effects of cortisol. (But, thankfully, those days are numbered—or have ended already!)

Spending time with dogs has been shown to reduce cortisol levels—both in you *and* the animal. It's a symbiotic benefit that helps explain why pet ownership has been such a valued experience for thousands of years.

Pickleball or Padel: Choose Your Addiction

Pickleball is a lot like an oversized version of ping-pong—although that isn't an International Pickleball Federation-endorsed description (and yes, such a federation does exist). It'll get you moving but it doesn't require the same range of motion as tennis. You can play even if you have mobility limitations, and particularly if your opponent is of approximately the same skill level.

There are a couple of reasons for this. One is that pickleball courts are about half the size of a tennis court. You aren't running to get the ball, and the striking motion is also easier on your joints. Tennis players hit the ball with astounding velocity, but pickleball favors a much gentler range of motion.It's perhaps for this reason that racquet sports are frequently recommended for older people. They're easy on the body and have been found to be the most effective sport for dropping mortality rates. Can't go wrong there.

Padel is also a racquet sport, but it's played on a unique court that's flanked on either side by glass enclosures. Players are allowed to bounce the ball off the glass walls, but the ball is only allowed to bounce one time before being returned.

While you may not have a padel court near you, that may change soon.

The game is becoming increasingly popular in the United States with new courts opening up all the time, and it's already incredibly popular in countries like Spain and Mexico (it actually originated in the latter nation).

Chair Yoga: Flexibility for All

Yoga is designed so that anyone can do it—*literally* anyone. Chair yoga is a modification that allows you to sit or use a chair for balance at all times. It's a great way for beginners or people with physical disabilities to gain confidence while exploring various poses, and all the typical yoga focuses remain. Chair yoga still allows you to focus on mind/body connectedness, breathing exercises, and your physical health. It's great for increasing your blood circulation, concentration, and joint health.

Yoga improves flexibility, balance, and endurance, but it also has mental health benefits. It's been shown to reduce stress and anxiety, and it's linked to lower instances of insomnia [9]. If you've been achy (an increasingly common issue as we near the golden years), yoga is a particularly effective way to address your pain, and it's often used as a way to strengthen back and neck muscles.

Stand-Up Paddleboarding: Fun on the Water

Often known as SUP, stand-up paddleboarding is a relatively accessible water activity suitable for people of various skill levels and physical abilities. It *does* require you to be able to stand up on your paddleboard, which can be challenging at first. However, most people get the hang of it surprisingly quickly.

Once you're on your feet, you use a paddle to propel yourself through the water. Steering is accomplished by changing the side and path of your strokes. Mechanically speaking, it's easy to start but difficult to master.

Physical demand can vary. A leisurely paddle around smooth waters may be relatively easy, while getting through choppier weather can be very challenging.

The great thing about paddleboarding is its adaptability. If you have physical limitations, you can often enjoy the sport with modifications, like kneeling instead of standing while you paddle. Some paddleboards are designed for stability, and inflatable boards provide a softer surface. Adaptive equipment, such as specialized paddles or assistive devices, can be utilized to accommodate other specific needs.

While watersports are associated with big price tags, paddleboarding is relatively affordable. Most of the equipment can be rented, and virtually any body of water will do. In fact, many people start out in pools because the conditions are more controlled. (Disregard the neighbors' stares—they're likely just trying to pick up some tips from your smooth moves.)

And if you're looking for a scenic paddleboard route, a great choice is the one on Lady Bird Lake (a reservoir on the Colorado River) that runs through downtown Austin, Texas. The water is calm, you get great views of the city, and you can rent a paddleboard right there on the lake downtown!

Home Workouts to Pump You Up

Luckily (especially those of us who are gym-shy), it's very easy to perform a wide range of exercises at home. Yoga and other forms of stretching can be done anywhere. There are also many guided video workouts available for free online, which can serve as a great way to find and learn exercises that can be done with things around the house. Basic recommendations include chair squats, pushups, situps, stationary bikes, treadmills, wall pilates, resistance band workouts, and tools like the TRX System (Total Resistance Exercises) suspension bands.

Before you begin a focused exercise routine, it's a good idea to speak with your doctor. They may have recommendations for how you should start and what techniques might be appropriate for you.

Dance Like Nobody's Watching

Dancing is one of those things that just makes you feel alive. You lock in with your dancing partner, allow yourselves to become hypnotized by the music, and glide to the rhythm of the beat. During those moments, you're fully present, and nothing else matters

as long as you know what you're doing! If that's not you (yet), know that anybody can learn with some practice and it's never too late to get started.

And the best part is that there's plenty of great dance types to choose from. Salsa, bachata, merengue, ballroom, the ol' country two-step…the possibilities are endless.

And it's not only fun—it's healthy, too!

A 2023 study reported the benefits of using dance to supplement or even replace more traditional forms of exercise [10]. While the study itself was conducted on children, the findings scale very naturally to the general population.

Dancing can raise your heart rate and boost your cardiovascular health in much the same way as any other form of vigorous exercise. However, the study also found that dancing has additional benefits not seen as consistently in other forms of physical activity.

Shaking your stuff can help improve confidence and self-esteem while also reducing the risk of cognitive decline. As an added bonus, it's also usually a social activity—which, of course, carries its own benefits (and who knows—if you're on the dating market, it just might help you meet your next romantic partner).

Dancing Styles for Every Fitness Level

Like yoga, dancing is endlessly adaptable. There are some chair-specific types of dancing that are perfect for people most comfortable remaining primarily seated. There are also many modifications for more traditional forms of dance.

You may also encounter senior-oriented dance classes at your local library or community center. If there are commercial studios where you live, you might consider reaching out to see what options they have available for people at your skill level—chances are they'll have classes suitable for you. If not, they'll almost surely be open to helping you find modifications to participate in their regular classes. After all, it's how they make their living. They win, you win.

Get Up & Boogie: Zumba Gold

Zumba is a workout style inspired by Latin dance. It's highly spirited and widely considered as a fun way to get your heart rate up. While it's only been around for about 20 years, Zumba has become enormously popular in a relatively short amount of time.

According to the Zumba brand website, more than 12 million people take classes *every week*. And they aren't all athletic or even physically fit; like most forms of dance, Zumba can be adjusted to fit your comfort level.

Finding Local Dance Classes & Socials

In addition to most dance studios offering classes particularly for seniors, all age groups are generally welcome to join any beginner dance classes as well, so you'll have plenty of options.

Below are a few tips for finding dance classes near you:

- Start by searching, "senior dance classes near me" on Google and see what you find.

- Look for local dance studios on Google as well to see what kinds of classes they offer. Keep your eye on beginner classes, as well as classes for seniors.

- Check in with local community centers, along with gym and fitness centers, and ask what type of senior dance classes they offer.

- Ask friends and family. You may have some loved ones that are into dance, or maybe you've seen a friend post about a dance class on social media.

Pedal to the Metal: Cycling Adventures

You definitely don't need to be a triathlete or Tour De France competitor to enjoy a good bit of cycling. And if you have joint pain, this may actually be the perfect sport for you.

The Arthritis Foundation names cycling as one of the best exercises for people struggling with joint pain. It's one of the most rigorous yet low-impact exercises out there, allowing you to get your heart rate up almost to the same extent you would on a lengthy run.

Another great thing about cycling is that it can be easily woven into a larger adventure. The United States has more than 18,000 miles of bike trails [11], and many of them are located in scenic locations. If you get really into cycling, you can plan trips around your new hobby, and even join groups within your community that ride together.

The following are a few amazing cycling trails that you and your friends can explore:

- **The Virginia Creeper Trailer (Virginia):** This 34-mile trail passes forests and farmlands along the beautiful WhiteTop Laurel River.

- **Cape Cod Trail (Massachusetts):** Stretching for 25 miles and following the former Old Colony Railroad, this trail passes through picturesque towns, salt marshes, and cranberry bogs. It also offers a beautiful view of the Cape Cod scenery.

- **The Napa Valley Vine Trail (California):** This 47-mile trail passes through California's famous wine country, making it a gorgeous choice in the fall.

- **Camino De Santiago (Spain):** Feeling really adventurous—and up for a flight across the Atlantic? This is an especially long trail, up to 485 miles depending on the route, but you don't need to do the whole thing in one shot! It starts in France and ends in

Spain, and it's also a famous religious pilgrimage route known all over the world.

Keep in mind, however, that bikes can be surprisingly expensive (though there are many affordable options available), so if you aren't ready to fully commit, consider renting a bike from a shop in your town. Many cities also have basic bikes that can be rented on the street using a phone app. While these units aren't suitable for major biking adventures, they can still be a fun way to get around town as you mull over whether this is the hobby for you.

Try These Fun Cycling Challenges

If you're interested in the idea of biking but need a little extra motivation, **we've put together a few challenges below that can spice up your ride:**

- **Beginner's Century Ride:** Aim to complete a 100-mile ride over the course of a month, breaking it down into smaller, manageable daily distances. It sounds like a lot, but keep in mind that miles go by *much* quicker on a bike than they do on foot.

- **Scenic Trail Exploration:** Discover local bike trails and aim to ride a new one each week, enjoying the beauty of nature and different landscapes. You may be able to find local bike riding groups that provide a list of great spots near you. These can be excellent resources for those just starting out.

- **Coffee Shop Tour:** Here's a novel (yet possibly **caffeinated)** idea—plan a series of rides to visit various local coffee shops. It's a great way to explore your community while rewarding yourself with a nice cup of coffee or tea.

Just Keep Swimming: Aquatic Exercises

Believe it or not, swimming is even more physically accessible than biking. It produces virtually no stress on your joints and works out all of your major muscle groups. Water aerobics classes are popular forms of exercise among senior citizens because they can be comfortably performed, even by those of us with arthritis or other forms of chronic pain.

And aside from actually swimming, below are a couple of common types of water aerobics you can try:

- **Water Walking or Marching:** This involves walking in the shallow end of the pool with the water level around waist height. The resistance of the water provides a gentle workout that aids cardiovascular health.

- **Water Aerobic Arm Curls:** For this exercise, stand in chest-deep water and hold a water dumbbell or pool noodle in each hand, then curl the dumbbells up to your shoulders.

Unfortunately, while swimming *is* physically accessible, there are some barriers to participation. Not everyone has easy access to a pool. If your city has a fitness center, you may be able to get an affordable membership. Start by looking for a local LA Fitness gym, as those are widespread across the US and usually have pools—along with affordable memberships.

Otherwise, see if you can find a comparable option in a nearby town. With a little bit of determination, you should be able to find an indoor pool within close proximity. These locations will also often have classes available for people at a wide range of skill levels. Have no fear—you'll fit right in no matter what level you're at.

Unconventional Workouts for the Adventurous

As has been made obvious thus far, many things can be considered exercise. What matters the most is that you stay within your comfort level—not taking on activities that might result in injury—and that you get your heart rate up.

When you move your body for an extended period of time, it improves blood circulation. This has the benefit of lowering your blood pressure and regulating your heart rate. These are very important for everyone, but especially for people who are at retirement age. While the average age for a heart attack is between 65 and 72, anyone can be at risk, and heart attacks experienced by people in their fifties have been on the rise for years [12].

Diversifying your approach to exercise is a great way to reduce that risk. When looking to hone your exercise routine, it's important to choose activities that you can comfortably fold into it.

Exercise is about habit, but how you choose to habitually engage in exercise has many forms. Below, we'll examine a few exercises you've possibly never even considered before.

Hula Hooping

While many people think of hula hooping as a kid's game (or perhaps a stereotypical Hawaiian tradition), it's actually a powerful way to exercise. It has many of the same health benefits as dancing because the range of motion can be very similar. It's also low-impact, making it a good choice for people who are trying to be mindful of their joint health.

Many instructional videos are available on the internet that can help get you started with this waist-twisting exercise.

Aqua Jogging

If you like the idea of running but don't want to pound your joints to sawdust, aquatic jogging is a great—albeit fairly strenuous—alternative. Pretty much exactly what it sounds like, aquatic jogging involves performing the same motions you use on a run—but rather in a pool.

If the pool you have access to is shallow enough, you can aqua jog easily in the lap lanes. In some rec centers or gyms, you may even encounter submerged, treadmill-like devices that allow you to perform this exercise in place.

Aerial Yoga

As mentioned earlier, yoga can basically be modified endlessly, and aerial yoga proves the point. It involves performing poses while suspended from a hammock-like device. It may sound a little silly (or maybe very silly), but there *are* proven benefits. Aerial yoga helps with joint decompression, making it a great fit for people experiencing discomfort.

It also may be more mentally engaging than regular yoga because it's so unique. Remember—any chance to stimulate your mind is beneficial. When you can kill two birds with one stone, all the better.

But if you've never tried yoga before, you may want to start with chair yoga before getting into the aerial variation—then again, it all depends how adventurous you're feeling!

Tai Chi: Gentle Movements, Big Health Benefits

While it can be used for self-defense, Tai Chi—a martial art originating in China—favors much slower and more deliberate motions than other forms of martial arts. It typically involves light physical contact and encourages motions that resemble yoga poses.

Tai Chi can provide a nice, gentle aerobic exercise, and it's a great way to strengthen your muscles in a low-stress environment. It's also excellent for relaxing. Because Tai Chi is all about deliberate motions, it can be used as an effective mindfulness activity, encouraging you to focus solely on how you are moving your body.

Finding Local Classes for the Latest Fitness Trends

There's always a new fitness fad, and while some of them are more compelling than others, it can be fun to sample what's out there.

You never know when you might stumble into the next trendy exercise like Zumba. If you're interested in trying new activities, research local fitness studios in your town. Chances are they stay on top of trending health concepts and find ways to introduce them into their studios.

Also ask friends and see what they're up to fitness wise. They may be trying something new that peaks your interest, too.

Not only is this a great way to stay fit but it's also fun—and *that's* the ultimate goal of any fitness endeavor. If you can find activities that keep you moving but don't feel like a chore, you'll ultimately find a lot more success (and stick with it).

Remember—staying active is a little like saving for retirement. Doing a little bit here and there is nice, but regularly putting in even a modest effort is better. Consistency is key. If you prioritize getting at least 30 minutes of physical activity a day, it'll help regulate your weight and improve your cardiovascular health.

Key Takeaways

- Daily activity helps your heart health, but it can also delay cognitive decline.

- Dance, Zumba, yoga, and many other popular health classes already have modifications available for people at every skill level.

- Exercises don't have to be boring or hard. Anything that gets your body moving for 30 to 60 minutes a day will be beneficial, so find hobbies that are rewarding and physically demanding.

- It all adds up. You can burn around 300 calories with 30 minutes of vigorous exercise. Commit to it daily to regulate your weight and enjoy improved health.

Chapter 4

Piña Coladas, Dating, Friendship & Singlehood: What's Your Style?

"You should be kissed often and by someone who knows how."
-quote from the film Gone with the Wind

Who are you going to spend your retirement with? That's the big question that weighs on many people's minds, even as they navigate the financial and health realities of their new lifestyle. The quote featured above from *Gone with the Wind* is popular, it's punchy, and a little sexy—but it has a fair bit of truth to it. In short, it's nice to be kissed, and it's very nice to be kissed by someone who knows what they're doing.

That doesn't mean that retired singles need to jump back into the world of dating—we're aware that it's not for everyone—but it does mean you should at least *think* about your romantic wants and needs.

In this section, we'll look at romance, singledom, friendship, and everything in between.

Rediscovering Romance: Modern Dating for Today's Seniors

If you've been out of romantic rotation for awhile, you may be surprised by how much things have changed. Remember the tech slogan, "There's an app for that?" It's actually never been more true. While there are still romantic partners who meet each other in person, it's more common than ever to find your partner through the online dating realm.

Below, we'll explore how you can safely and effectively navigate both the virtual and in-person dating landscape.

Playing the Field After 50

As a senior, you likely don't have the same patience for fleeting romance, and especially not for pre-date jitters. It's possible that dating has changed so much since you were last in the game that you don't even know where to begin.

But does the modern landscape even *have* an outlet for the after-50 crowd? You better believe it! There are *plenty* of essential dating apps that are designed for people of a certain age (like ours). The diversity of options makes it easy to narrow down and get specific. For example, there are apps specifically tailored for people of certain religious denominations, and also professional, educational, and racial backgrounds.

Online dating isn't the only way to play the field after 50—but it may not feel like the most natural way either. And that's okay, because it's all about finding what works for *you*. In the next section, we'll delve into the world of virtual dating. And a little after that, we'll provide information for people who like to meet their romantic partners the old-fashioned way. You can even mix up your game with a little bit of both. Variety, as they say, is the spice of life—so keep your options open and fresh!

Online Dating Platforms: Swiping for Love

Online dating used to be a punchline—the last resort for people who can't find love anywhere else. However, it's been, oh…about 20 years since that has had even the tiniest bit of truth to it. In fact, more than half of all singles currently have an online dating profile.

To be fair, the number does dip slightly for people trying to find love at a more mature age. Pew Research Center found that only about 20% of people aged 50 and over use online dating [14], but that definitely doesn't mean it isn't a great way to find love. For one thing, 20% still accounts for a *lot* of people. For another, the stat most likely reflects habit more than anything else.

The 50-plus community is much more used to meeting people in-person than today's 20-somethings. Let's have a glance at a handful of apps that might be worth exploring if you'd like to give swiping for love a try. And if you don't understand the reference, **it's only because you haven't tried the apps yet, so let's dig in:**

- **eHarmony:** This platform is well-known for its algorithms, which delve deeply into personality traits and preferences to provide optimal matches.

- **Silver Singles:** Tailored exclusively for singles over 50, Silver Singles provides a user-friendly platform with a focus on genuine connections, fostering a community seeking serious relationships.

- **Our Time:** This option is designed for the over-50 crowd in every way, with a straightforward interface and user-friendly features designed to make it easy to find love and companionship.

- **Senior Match:** This one brands itself around helping retirees find people to spend their golden years with. If you look at their site, you'll see ad copy all about finding someone to travel the world with. Because of that focus, it may be particularly effective for people who want a serious retirement relationship.

Then you've got the more widespread dating apps. The age on these skew a bit younger, **but there are plenty of 50- and 60-plus people on these platforms:**

- **Hinge:** This is the most premium-feeling of the three apps listed here. It's the least spammy, and also the one with which you're most likely to find quality matches and dates.

- **Bumble:** This app is designed so that the women must message first, which puts an interesting spin on things!

- **Tinder:** The most spammy of the three apps, but Tinder is also the oldest and most common, so it could be worth a try. Just be aware of the potential bot accounts out there. If the account has no bio, or looks a little fake, it's likely too good (or too bad) to be true.

Keep in mind that the way a website or app brands itself isn't necessarily the way individual users behave. People tend to pick dating sites that align with their specific wants and interests, but you ultimately never know who'll be online. That's why proper precautions are so important.

It's also a good idea to choose a few different dating apps or websites— don't put all your focus on just one, or else you may be closing yourself off from meeting the right romantic partner. Of course, don't overwhelm yourself, but a solid mix could be to choose one or two of the sites and one or two of the apps.

Note, however, that photos are *everything* when it comes to online dating. The better yours are, the more matches and interest you'll receive, and the higher quality of potential mates you can date. So, if this is something that you're going to take seriously, **aim to do the following in terms of photos:**

- **Use Professional Photos:** Don't use a random mishmash of past photos that were randomly taken—these *never* work well. And no selfies! Be intentional, find a professional photographer, and do things right. It'll definitely be worth your time. You can find some great photographers in your area on sites like Snappr and Thumbtack.

- **Mind Your Backgrounds:** The backgrounds of your photos make a *big* difference in their overall feel and how dating prospects will view you. Avoid the studio backgrounds (these feel staged), and definitely don't take photos in your house. Generally, city backdrops and landscapes, along with upscale lounges, have a more premium feel. Ask your photographer if they have any recommendations, but it's a good idea to scout out some of these areas and venues yourself before you do a photoshoot.

- **Get Style Feedback:** Conduct some style research, or consider bringing on a style consultant who can help make sure that your outfits look great before your photos. Matching patterns and colors (as well as proper fit!) are the biggest keys.

Sure, it may feel a little funny or out of your comfort zone going to these lengths. But remember that online dating is a competition, and great photos will catapult you to the top 5% and help you meet the best potential romantic partners out there. Plus, you can grab some great photos in the span of just a few hours that'll last you for years!

Staying Safe: Tips for Online Dating

There's a reason the term "catfishing" has become an actual verb in popular vernacular. Online spaces aren't always safe. People can lie easier from behind a screen than they can in-person, and it can be justifiably frightening to meet up with someone for the first time who you've only spoken to online.

Despite the challenges and the uncomfortable aspects of online dating, it's something that millions of people all over the planet do safely every day. **Here's how to safely become a catch online without putting yourself at risk:**

- **Guard Personal Information:** Refrain from sharing sensitive details, such as your home address, phone number, or financial information.

- **Use a Reputable Platform:** Choose well-established online dating platforms with positive reviews and a commitment to user safety.

- **Be Wary of Red Flags:** Pay attention to potential signs of suspicious behavior, such as someone pressuring you for personal information or money. Report and block users displaying inappropriate or harmful conduct.

- **Choose Public Meeting Places:** Select public locations like cafes, restaurants, or bars for initial meetings, prioritizing your safety. And always inform a friend or family member about your plans and location.

- **Trust Your Instincts:** If something feels uncomfortable or off during the date, trust your instincts and consider ending the encounter. Having a backup plan, like a friend on standby, can provide added security.

- **Stay Sober:** Limit alcohol consumption during the date to remain alert and aware. Also, avoid leaving drinks unattended to prevent the risk of tampering. Better safe than sorry, as they say.

If you're thinking, "This is tricky stuff…dating didn't used to come with so many disclaimers," you're right—it didn't. But keep in mind that people have *always* taken reasonable precautions when getting to know strangers—those precautions just look a little different now.

When you were 19 and meeting people out in the world, maybe you didn't need to have dating advice laid out in such clear terms, but the fact that you've made it to retirement age suggests that you were reasonably attuned to the risks!

Times have changed, but many fundamentals haven't. Most people are decent, but some aren't. By taking sensible precautions, you can enjoy online dating without any significant problems.

Budget-Friendly Dating Ideas

Maybe you *would* like to date, but you don't want to blow all your hard-earned retirement savings on wine and flowers—especially on a number of first encounters that might not go anywhere. But there are plenty of ways to enjoy affordable, romantic dating activities.

Remember—as you're still getting to know someone, it's best to choose public activities. Sometimes that may mean spending a bit of money on dinners out, but even in these situations, you don't need to spend a ransom.

Consider a casual dessert date during which you get to know someone over ice cream. Maybe you'd rather laugh over lattes or connect over a cocktail. You get the idea. You don't have to buy a stranger a romantic dinner to enjoy a decent date. There are countless ways to get to know someone in a public setting for ten dollars—or even less!

Once you're a little more comfortable with that person, you'll find that there are even more options for affordable dates—particularly when you decide that you're okay with inviting them into your home.

Below are a few more affordable date ideas for various stages in your relationships:

- **Picnic in the Park:** Enjoying a lunch or even dinner in a local park is a budget-friendly date idea that allows for a relaxed atmosphere and quality time together surrounded by nature. Bringing homemade snacks adds a personal touch while keeping costs low—and it shows your potential partner that you're no slouch in the kitchen.

- **Outdoor Movie Night at Home:** Opting for an outdoor film in your backyard or balcony provides a cozy and intimate setting without the expense of an actual cinema. Movie projectors are surprisingly affordable and easy to use, allowing you to create somewhat of a drive-in experience from the comfort of your home.

- **Visit a Free Event or Exhibition:** Attend local community events, art exhibitions, or cultural festivals. These are often free and give you and your partner the opportunity to explore or develop shared interests.

- **Cooking Together at Home:** Cooking a meal together at home is a cost-effective and fun date option. Choose a new recipe to try. Make a big mess. It'll be just like a movie montage—and maybe your first romantic scene together!

Finding Local Social & Dating Opportunities

If you'd rather stay offline for your romantic enterprises, there are lots of ways to meet people out there in the real world—just like the "olden" days before everything got so techy. In fact, that's where the majority of people in our age group will be most comfortable. Remember when we mentioned earlier that 80% of people over 50 look for love offline? That's because there are plenty of social opportunities in which to meet them.

Once you open yourself up to the idea of dating, you'll find that there's the potential for it *everywhere*. For example, if you're planning on taking up one of the hobby groups (cycling, hiking, dance, etc.) mentioned in the last chapter, those could be excellent ways to meet people your age with common interests. Instead of tripping your way through first-date small talk (often a challenge!), you can start on some comfortable ground and then build on it.

If you don't have that kind of social outlet, there are many other ways to meet interesting and available retirees. Some communities will have social events specifically geared toward giving people in our age group the opportunity to mingle. These can generally be found at community centers, YMCAs, churches, and so on.

Consider also:

- **Speed Dating:** These are quick micro-interactions in which you spend a few minutes each with many other single people. No pressure, though—contact information is only exchanged in situations where two people are mutually interested.

- **Blind Dates:** Blind dates can be awkward, but they certainly aren't the worst way to meet people—and they can actually be a bit exciting. They usually happen because someone in your social circle feels that they know someone else who'll be a good match for you. It's a little like online dating but with a solid Google review, so to speak, endorsing the person you'll be meeting.

- **Spontaneous Connection:** Naysayers aside—it *does* still happen! You're going about your day when suddenly you meet someone you think is interesting in line at a coffee shop or browsing the aisles of your local library. While spontaneous connections have become rarer these days, they're still a nice and pleasingly romantic way to meet someone special, so be on the look-out!

73

Long-Term Relationships: Reigniting the Spark

Those of us entering retirement who are already in a long-term relationship are sometimes surprised to find that our union has become more challenging than originally assumed. You still love the one you're with, but you're just *so* used to seeing them all day, every day. All of a sudden, you find that your routines are colliding in ways they never have before.

It's an adjustment period—and not unlike moving in with someone for the first time. But instead of learning that the person you care about leaves their dirty socks on the bathroom floor, you discover instead that you don't quite know how to find the right romantic balance anymore now that you're together all the time.

It's natural, it's normal, and it's navigable. Below, we'll explore how to reignite the spark.

Keeping the Flame Alive: Date Nights & Surprises

Date nights establish a sense of occasion that domestic life often lacks. It's hard to feel romantically inclined toward a person all the time when you're constantly bumping up against their habits, routines, and even flaws (hey—we all have them) But on date nights, there's an extra effort and more attention paid to the little things. No one leaves the door open while they sit on the toilet, and no one talks about household finances or chores that need to be done. Refreshing!

The focus shifts toward having a nice time with the person you care about. As mentioned earlier, these outings can be affordable. Think about how nice you'd feel if the person you love surprised you with a picnic in the park or a spontaneous ice cream date.

74

You can also keep the flame alive yourself by doing that for *them*. Once you establish the habit of a little spontaneity, you may find that it becomes a regular feature in your romantic life. Keep in mind that date nights and surprises don't have to involve huge gestures—although, as you'll see in a moment, sometimes they can be fantastic ways to rekindle the flame.

But first, **some simpler options could involve:**

- **Bringing Home Something Special:** This could be flowers, chocolates, or even a snack you know that they're particularly fond of. It only costs you a few dollars but it lets your special someone know that you were thinking of them.

- **Re-Enact an Earlier Date:** This is a huge win! Who says the romantic days of your youth are behind you? For a little spice, take a trip down memory lane, re-creating to the best of your abilities a date from yesteryear. It's fun, it's romantic, and it might just conjure up feelings of what it's like to be young and in love. You can't put a price tag on that.

- **Do Something They Usually Handle Themselves:** This could be almost anything, but it won't go unnoticed. Filling up their car with gas. Mopping the kitchen. Doing the dishes. It's another easy way to remind your someone that you care about them. And they might even (hopefully) decide to return the favor!

Hot Air Balloon Rides & Other Romantic Adventures

As mentioned above, bigger displays of affection are also great if you have the time and resources. While ordinary gestures of kindness and love are a nice way to show someone that you care, more elaborate dates are a fantastic way to create new memories and simply reignite your excitement for life—and each other.

Hot air balloons are a unique date option, but there are plenty of other ways to try something new and a bit grandiose in a safe but exciting environment:

- **Zip-Lining Adventure:** Experience an exhilarating day by going zip-lining together. It provides an adrenaline rush and a shared sense of excitement while enjoying scenic views.

- **Helicopter Tour:** Embark on a ride in the skies for a thrilling aerial perspective of your surroundings. While this may sound ludicrously expensive, it's likely more affordable than you might guess, and many cities have helicopter tour services available. It'll possibly run you around $200 to $300, but you may decide that it's money well-spent for a once-in-a-lifetime experience.

- **Sailing or Yachting Excursion:** Rent a sailboat or a yacht for a stunning day on the water. Depending on the aquatic environment of your community, you may be able to make a whole day out of it. Also, many lake towns will have restaurants and attractions accessible from the water.

- **Paragliding or Hang Gliding:** Terrifying? Maybe, but what better way to remember your love for someone than to spend an hour fearing desperately for your life by their side? This is a great option if you're both up for a bit of a thrill!

This all may feel a little frivolous. After all, you may already be at the age at which you can get discounted movie theater tickets. If you've never climbed onto a hot air balloon or gone zip-lining before, you may scoff at being struck by the urge now.

However, there are a couple of things that may change your mind. The first is that all the activities above are reasonably safe for people of almost any physical condition. Even zip-lining, which may sound insane to you, basically requires sitting still and letting gravity do the work for you.

The second thing? Going on adventures has proven psychological benefits [15]. A research survey conducted during the pandemic indicated that adventure-based recreation activities were one of the most effective ways of dealing with feelings of social isolation and general anxiety—things that retirees deal with routinely.

Adventurous activities also tend to help solidify memories much more vividly than, say, going out to a decent restaurant you've been to numerous times already. When you get to a certain age, it can be hard to find experiences that feel exciting and new again.

However, if you're willing to think outside the box a little, you'll find that there's an entire world of adventure waiting to be explored. So why not step into it with someone you love and trust?

Finding Common Ground: Sharing Interests & Hobbies

As you've likely determined, retirement is largely what Taylor Swift might refer to as your "hobby and interests era." (It's okay if you didn't understand that reference—we barely get it ourselves.)

But the fact remains that you're likely going to be exploring your interests at a much deeper level than you were previously used to. This can become a personal silo of sorts, in which you engage with something you care about all by yourself. There's nothing wrong with that, but consider the pleasures of bringing your significant someone into the fold.

They don't have to become as passionate about, say, model trains as you are (because let's face it—that's a fairly tall order), but you can at least teach them the terminology and show them what you get up to in the basement at all hours of the day.

In exchange, you can ask questions about their stamp collection or find out about the latest and greatest in the world of gardening. You may even discover mutual passions—and it's always more enjoyable to explore your interests with someone you love.

Other times, you won't quite get where they're coming from. "Stamps…still square, I see…and ah, yes—someone has licked them. Fascinating…" you may think as they show you their collection. But it's all about getting a glimpse into their world and sharing something that's important to you in the process.

Creating Your Couples Bucket List

Naturally, now is also a great time to think about all the things you want to see and do with your significant other during your lifetimes. Perhaps travel the country in an RV, galavant around Europe, or learn a second language together. There are no right or wrong ways to plan your dream retirement life.

It is, of course, important to be realistic about what you can afford on your budget. However, as explained often throughout this book, joy is accessible to everyone regardless of their financial means. **For example:**

- **Regional Road Trips:** Plan a series of car journeys throughout your area to explore nearby towns, scenic routes, and hidden gems. This gradual exploration allows you to uncover the beauty of your own region at a relaxed pace.

- **Historic Landmark Quest:** Create a list of historical landmarks within driving distance and visit them gradually. Immerse yourselves in the rich history of your surroundings, appreciating the architecture and stories behind each landmark. There are 2,600 of them in the United States, many of which may be closer than you might assume.

- **Culinary Tour of Local Gems:** Explore the food scene of nearby towns and cities. You can make an entire day out of getting lunch at a great little hole-in-the-wall three towns over.

- **Cultural Festival Circuit:** Identify cultural festivals or events happening throughout the year in your region. Depending on how much territory you're willing to cover, you'll likely be surprised by how much is going on within a couple hundred miles of your home.

Affordable Ways to Keep the Romance Alive

You can also fill your days with romance without ever spending very many pennies. One of the best ways to generate excitement is to experience new things together—that's kind of the idea behind the adventurous suggestions offered a little earlier in the book. However, you don't have to defy gravity in order to keep things spicy.

Instead, look for little things you can do to keep things interesting. Invite your person out for a glass of wine under the stars one summer evening. Buy a couple of canvases and paint one another—the results may not be worthy of the Louvre (or even your local flea market), but you'll definitely have fun doing it.

All those clubs and special interest groups mentioned previously are also great ways to branch out with your romantic partner. Whether the two of you decide to take up cycling or local history together, shared activities are always a fantastic way to reignite your connection.

The Art of Connection: Building & Maintaining Meaningful Friendships

Sometimes, a little more emphasis is put on romance than is necessary. Yes, it's an exciting form of a relationship, and one that most people have at least some degree of interest in. After all, Shakespeare didn't write tragedies about friends who just really liked hanging out.

But while love stories get all the ink, friendships remain an enduring and important social outlet that you should nurture as much as possible, and retirement is an excellent time in which to do it.

Friends: The Family You Choose

Friends are an irreplaceable support system, precisely for the fact that they're *chosen*. While family is obviously important—irreplaceable, even—they're ultimately made up of people who were given to you. But you actually found your friends (or they found you). And while famous short story writer O. Henry claimed that no true friendships are accidental, there's at the very least a happy sort of magic that takes place when two people decide to be a part of each other's lives for no other reason than that they care.

Friends are the family that you choose. But as we get older, we may realize that our social connections have dwindled or grown stale. People move away or pass on. Other relationships simply get neglected over the years as we focus on work or family. It's sad to realize, only at retirement, that our social circles have shrunk.

However, that doesn't mean that you're out of options. There are plenty of ways to re-ignite old friendships and create new ones.

Tips for Making New Friends

"Oh no," you're possibly thinking. "I've seen a lot in my life, and the last thing I want is to enter retirement feeling like the new kid on the playground." If you feel uncomfortable or even anxious about the idea of trying to make new friends, it's completely understandable—and common. It's frightening no matter how old you are or how many social connections you've made in your life.

There are many ways to make friends—ways that feel natural and easy. **For example:**

- **Local Clubs or Classes:** Join groups or courses related to your interests, whether it's painting, gardening, photography, or basically anything else you can think of. Local community centers often host groups where you can connect with like-minded people.

- **Local Charities:** Offer your time and skills to local charities or organizations. Volunteering not only allows you to give back but also provides an opportunity to meet people who share a similar commitment to community service.

- **Attend Local Gatherings:** Participate in community events, town hall meetings, or neighborhood gatherings. These informal settings offer a chance to meet the people living all around you.

There are even online platforms designed for connecting with people in your community. Meetup is a social forum that helps connect people with similar interests. And Bumble, which is primarily known as a dating app, also has a feature for people who simply want to make friends.

Remember—consistency is key. The more often you put yourself out there, the more likely it is that you'll make meaningful connections.

Creating New Memories with Old Friends

Discovering new experiences with old friends is a great way to breathe new life into relationships that have gone flat or simply become a little too set in their ways. While you likely won't be trying to win a kiss at the end of the night with your friend (although, hey—you never know), the concept is not dissimilar from trying to add excitement to an old relationship.

Try new things together! Obviously, the specifics of what that entails will depend on what your relationships currently look like. If you and your friends are the "sit around and watch sports" crowd, consider getting out in the fresh air. Hike. Fish. Golf.

There are also lots of fun and trendy activities that you can pay to participate in. For example, escape rooms or ax-throwing classes are great options—they're quirky activities that can add a little excitement to your routine.

Affordable Friendship Activities: Fun Doesn't Have to Be Expensive

Friendship is free—as it should be. While there are lots of ways to spend money with your friends, you certainly don't have to. Hosting a night of cards, trivia, or other games can be a fun way to enjoy time with people you care about without spending any money at all.

Many physical activities like going out for bike rides or enjoying lengthy walks are also free of charge. If you'd like to get something regular going, consider starting a book group or a photography club. The specifics, of course, are ultimately for you to decide. Playing into your friend group's shared interests is always a winning strategy, but don't be afraid to suggest new activities as well. Who knows—you and your friends might just stumble into your next shared passion.

Finding Local Events & Meetups

You'll most likely find that your community is full of opportunities to meet new people. In fact, there are likely so many opportunities that it'll be hard to decide where you should begin. Start by looking as close to your home as possible and then branch out from there—this will help make sure that you're being thorough while also illuminating just how easy it can be to find solid opportunities.

One of the first things you might discover is that your own neighborhood has social opportunities. This could take the form of a homeowners association (they're generally more interesting than they sound) or even a neighborhood walking, hiking, gardening, or beautification group.

As you expand your search, you'll also likely discover opportunities within your wider city. Maybe the church you attend has opportunities for older adults to mingle, or perhaps your town community center has classes or mixers. Look into it! You'll almost certainly find that there's a lot out there that you had no idea about.

The Joys of Sociable Singlehood

You can absolutely live a full life without being romantically attached to anyone, and the joys of social singlehood are vast. You don't need to worry about anyone else's schedule. You always know what's in the refrigerator. And, possibly most important, no one's hogging the covers.

Unfortunately, it can be hard to find social or cultural references that reflect the rewards that come from enjoying time to yourself. However, with the right perspective, you can fully take advantage of and enjoy life as a single adult.

Self-Love Isn't Selfish: Prioritizing *You*

There's a big difference between being selfish and taking care of yourself. Think about what flight attendants say before take-off on an airplane. In the event of an emergency, you're always supposed to secure your own safety before helping anyone else. It's not because you're more important than the child sitting next to you (although that might depend strictly on how well-behaved they were during the flight), but it does mean that you won't be any good to the collective if you're slumped over in your seat from oxygen deprivation.

This is true in other situations as well. If you're burned out, under a lot of stress, or simply unhappy, you won't be much help to your friends, family, or community. Self-love means prioritizing your needs—after all, no one else is going to do it for you. **Forms of self-love can include:**

- **Taking Care of Yourself:** Eat right. Get enough sleep. Exercise. Behaviors that keep you healthy require consistent attention, so make them a priority in your schedule.

- **Noting the Way You Feel:** Use mindfulness techniques to monitor your feelings. You may notice tension or other challenging sensations that require a little extra attention.

- **Exploring Things, You Care About:** Exploring your hobbies and interests is *not* inherently selfish. Taking time for activities that make you happy will improve your mood and mental health.

Personal Growth: Discovering Your Favorite Activities & Interests

You're never too old to get to know yourself better. Giving yourself the time to explore new activities and interests in retirement is an amazing way to discover joys you never even knew existed before. While this certainly isn't the sole domain of single retirees, if you're not romantically attached to anyone, you're uniquely positioned to develop your schedule in a way that focuses specifically on things you care about. And that's a pretty beautiful thing.

Try to engage as fully as you can with your hobbies, and adding structure to your routine is a great way to do this. For example, if you want to get really into bird watching, find multiple ways to build it into your schedule. Wake up early to record observations. Schedule in time to read up on birds in the afternoon. Develop a list of books, documentaries, and podcasts you'd like to explore.

There are lots of ways to engage with new hobbies, all of which can be very rewarding when you give them your full attention. And now that you're not heading into work every day, it's prime time!

Finding Local Social & Hobby Groups

While you're exploring your hobbies, don't forget to look into the social potential of your new interest. As mentioned earlier, local hobby groups are a great way to meet like-minded people. Not only will you meet new friends but you might also benefit from a little extra structure now that your days are a bit more loose. Any group you join will most likely have programming that allows you to find additional ways to explore what you love.

There are so many ways to find social fulfillment as a retiree. Whether you're interested in romance, social outlets, self-love, or a combination of all three, you'll find plenty of options to connect with the wider world in your sunset years.

Key Takeaways

- It's easier than ever for single adults of every age to meet romantic partners safely. Some dating services are specifically designed for people in our age group. Virtually all of them have filters that allow you to state and refine your preferences.

- Spontaneity and adventure are excellent ways to refresh old relationships or even friendships. Try something new with the people you care about!

- Local life is a great way to explore free or affordable social activities. Your town may have a surprising number of free social activities that you never even knew about.

- Whether you're single or romantically attached, there are countless ways to explore your interests and passions. Prioritizing the things you care about—finally!—is a phenomenal way to add joy and fulfillment to your life.

Chapter 5

Tech-Savvy Seniors: Exploring the Digital Frontier

"A computer once beat me at chess, but it was no match for me at kickboxing."

-Emo Phillips, actor and comedian

Emo Phillips rather poignantly summarized the complexities of our relationship with digital technology as a species. It can be fun and joyous—and also terribly frustrating.

As we're becoming well aware of at our age, we need to have an attitude of continuous learning to fully enjoy and engage with digital technology. And for a generation who largely grew up on typewriters (maybe a word processor if we were lucky), that's not always an enticing offer.

Two things to keep in mind: Continuous learning keeps your mind sharp and fresh, and digital technology can open up entire new worlds.

In this chapter, we'll explore the pleasures of digital life at any age (but primarily ours).

Technology for Not-So-Twilighters

Digital technology may not feel like your forte, but the basics are more approachable than many tech-wary people realize. Keep in mind that these tech companies are trying to maximize their profits, and so they design things specifically to be used by the widest possible number of people. Once you wade into the world of digital technology, you'll most likely find it more approachable than you initially thought.

Below, we'll look at how you can safely and comfortably explore standard digital tools, including mobile devices and internet basics.

Mastering Mobile Devices & Internet Basics

We all easily remember the days when mobile phones didn't exist at all. Was life easier then? Was it better? It was certainly less complicated in terms of gadget-learning, that's for certain. Because not only do cell phones exist now but it seems that some evil-doer went and glued them into everyone's hands. And with frequent updates and advances, we're forced to *learn* about them—constantly!

Contrary to what the kids seem to believe, you certainly don't need to keep a smartphone four inches in front of your face at all times to enjoy digital technology. However, understanding how to properly use them makes it easier to connect with distant friends and family while also opening the door to unlimited knowledge and entertainment.

The following are the most basic steps for using your devices and internet connection safely:

- **Familiarize Yourself with Your Device:** While it may feel overwhelming to dive right in, taking a few moments to explore the settings and layout of your device will help a great deal. Trial and error is a great teacher. Also, feel free to ask for help at the store where you purchased your device—they'll be able to provide you with basic recommendations that align with what you hope to accomplish.

- **Get Your Firewalls Up:** This sounds more exciting than it actually is, but firewalls are software programs that protect your devices from viruses. Many phones and tablets are pre-programmed with safety technology, so you won't have to worry about that. However, PCs usually require third-party antivirus support. Norton, McAfee, and Avast are popular and easy-to-use options to keep your data and documents secure.

- **Learn How to Back Up Your Stuff:** You don't need to understand the cloud or how it works to use it effectively—many of us still can't seem to grasp the concept that all our precious virtual belongings exist somewhere "out there." But in a nutshell, backing up your information ensures that you'll never lose access to the photos, videos, and other digital resources that you treasure. Backing up your information also makes it incredibly easy to set up future devices. All the information you need will be there—always—with a few easy clicks.

Maintaining Your Privacy & Identifying Online Scams

In the spring of 2021, the Health Service Executive of Ireland, the nation's digital healthcare network, was hacked by a group of Russian cyber terrorists known as "Wizard Spider." The group managed to completely lock Ireland out of its own network. Hundreds of people had their personal information leaked, and the damage took weeks as well as many millions of dollars to repair.

They did this by tricking an employee into opening a virus-packed spreadsheet that had been sent to them in the form of an email.

Such a small mistake with such catastrophic results. But those are the risks when it comes to online safety. Hackers are like mice—they need just the tiniest point of entry to gain access to your system.

But let's not scare ourselves unnecessarily. Knowledge is power, and so being aware is one of the best ways to keep yourself safe. **Best practices include:**

- Keeping your firewalls active and up to date.

- Considering multi-factor identification protections. These require multiple methods of identity verification (text, email, and password) to access your accounts.

- Avoiding websites that seem fishy (your firewall will most likely automatically flag suspicious sites).

- Only opening emails from people or companies you know and trust.

Tech Newbie Tips & Tricks

Once you've figured out how to remain safe online and you know how to keep your information backed up, the next steps are largely determined by what you hope to accomplish. If you don't expect to do much online, you may simply look for easier ways to navigate your devices.

This could involve selecting a few key apps that make life easier. Maybe a fitness tracker app so that you can monitor those health metrics mentioned earlier, or a GPS app, with which you can set about exploring the country with ease.

You might also look for ways to simplify digital technology tasks. For example, most smartphones have voice commands that make it incredibly easy to pull up information, send messages, make calls, and much more.

And guess where you can find a plethora of information on how to accomplish—well, almost anything—with your internet-capable device? Surprise, surprise! It's online.

The thing that makes digital tools seem so unapproachable for people who haven't used them before is that they can do *too* much, and so the entire experience can become overwhelming. But once you understand what you want out of your device, it's easy to find resources that'll help you accomplish it.

Finding Local Technology Classes & Workshops

If you want to deepen your understanding of technology in a more organized environment and with others, look for classes and workshops in your community. Many libraries will offer regular courses for people at every skill level, and these opportunities are great because they're free!

You may also find similar opportunities at your community college or provided by various organizations within your area.

Classes and workshops are excellent because they provide a dynamic environment in which you can ask questions and meet people who may have backgrounds similar to your own. And if you're feeling befuddled by the latest tech, you can look around the room and think, "Well, we're all in this together." Strength in numbers!

Digital Diversions & Social Media

It's actually funny when you think about it—most of the world walks around with supercomputers right in their pockets. And what do we use them for? Cat videos, to name just one of many silly uses. All those people you see walking around with phones glued to their faces aren't saving the world. They're more likely to be exploring all manner of digital entertainment that are never more than a click or two away.

But, advantageously, the internet is thankfully home to a vast library of free or very affordable ways to keep yourself entertained. Below, we'll look at some popular ways to keep yourself occupied online when you need a break from the other retirement hobbies and activities outlined within this book.

Podcasts: Audio Entertainment & Enlightenment

Podcasts are a little like radio shows, but absolutely anyone can (and seemingly does) make them and put them out into the world. Some have really high budgets and high production values, while others are fairly low-fi—recorded in someone's house using inexpensive microphones and editing software. The world has truly become a global village when someone can sit in their basement and broadcast their thoughts to millions of people.

Below are some podcasting tips to get you started on listening in:

- If you have a hobby or interest, rest assured that there's most definitely a podcast about it. In fact, you'll most likely find that there are so many podcasts that you don't know where to get started. Explore a few shows until you find one (or more) that interest you.

- If you really like a celebrity, they very possibly have a podcast. And if they don't, there's a good chance that they've at least been interviewed on one.

- If you have any kind of a goal, there are podcasts available out there to help you reach it. From fitness to mindfulness to simply learning something new, your options are virtually unlimited.

Do keep in mind that, because there sometimes aren't quality gatekeepers in the world of podcasting, you do need to take many of them with a grain of salt. Look for shows that are made by people with established credentials in the topic you're interested in.

Learning New Skills on YouTube

If podcasting is amateur radio, YouTube is amateur TV (although many videos on the platform are *very* professionally done these days). The same rules apply as with podcasts—there's content available in every subject area. The production quality and accuracy of the information will vary considerably based on the source, but the number of options available to you will be almost unlimited.

It certainly helps to have a goal in mind. For example, if you want to learn chair yoga, you'll find entire channels dedicated only to that. Again, for basically any topic you can think of, you'll almost certainly find a

YouTube channel covering it. Use this platform to engage more deeply with your hobbies and interests, but always look for the most credible sources you can.

If you're just learning the YouTube ropes, it may help to search channels established by recognizable brands. For example, if you want to learn how to take on basic home improvement projects around the house, you might want to take a look at Home Depot's channel.

Digital Dollars: Getting to Know Cryptocurrency

Understanding the ins and outs of cryptocurrency could very easily fill its own book. We won't go to that extent here, but at the most basic level, you can think of it as digital currency. It's supported by a digital ledger of sorts called "blockchain," which provides transparency and safety to transactions.

Some people have found tremendous financial success investing in crypto. There's a famous story about an early Bitcoin investor who left his pizza guy a Bitcoin tip that was, at the time, worth just a few dollars, but is now valued into the millions.

Obviously, that's a rare situation, but it *does* reflect crypto's interesting potential.

The days of 1,000xing your portfolio are likely over. But with new tools like the Bitcoin ETF, it's easier to invest in crypto than ever before, and many people are starting to add it as 1 to 2% of their portfolios. It's an asymmetric bet, but of course you'll want to do your own research before investing in anything. As with everything else in this world, learn as much as you can and then proceed with caution.

Either way, crypto can be a fun thing to dabble in and learn more about. If you do decide to get into it, just don't invest anything you can't afford to lose!

Insta Gratification: Sharing Photos & Stories

Social media is a fantastic way to keep connected with friends and family members, and everyone has their own approach to how they use it. Some people keep silent accounts with which they don't post but rather use them to simply keep an eye on what their friends and family are up to.

Other people use their accounts as a way to share updates or images with those who are interested, and some others post every thought that comes into their head—whether their audience likes it or not). There's no wrong way to do social media (except for that last one—some things are meant for "inside voice" only).

Here's a breakdown of the most popular social media sites:

- **Facebook:** Great for community building and connecting with loved ones, whether current or from the past (yep—your old high school flame is likely on there, so proceed with caution!). You'll also find special groups built around unique interests. Facebook posts usually involve a combination of text, images, and videos.

- **X:** Formerly known as Twitter, X is a primarily text-based social media site used to provide short, punchier messages to communicate your own or others' thoughts with the world.

- **Instagram:** This app is focused almost entirely on images and videos (known as Stories or Reels). While posts are usually captioned with accompanying text, it's the pictures and clips that get all the attention.

- **TikTok:** A primarily video-based platform well known for short, punchy clips. Most of the content is designed to be entertaining or even funny (and sometimes its creators fail in this pursuit—everyone wants to be famous!), but there's also some educational content available.

- **Pinterest:** This is like a bulletin board montage but in digital form. You can use it to "pin" things that you're interested in and make plans for the future. Never too late to start a vision board of sorts!

Online Gaming & Virtual Reality Adventures

Gaming can be a fun way for people of all ages to unwind. You don't have to be like your bloodthirsty grandchildren, paving a crimson path on their Call of Duty adventures, to enjoy video games. There are many educational or otherwise mentally stimulating games to keep you occupied.

Finding Fun & Friends in Digital Spaces

Many online games have a social component built right into them, and sometimes you interact with other players directly. Those poor soldiers your grandchildren take down in Call of Duty are most likely being controlled by another player somewhere in the world, which adds a fascinating global feel to the experience. This sure ain't no game of 80s'-era Pong!

Even brain teasers may have a social component—for example, you might play a game that has a virtual leaderboard. The competitive element makes games more addictive, so do be careful that your other priorities aren't being thrown by the wayside. It's alarmingly easy to do!

Sometimes, this social component will include communication features. This can be an exciting way to play, allowing you to make virtual friends from all over the world, as mentioned above. You do, of course, need to keep all the usual internet rules in mind. Never disclose sensitive information online, avoid suggestions to meet up in person, and never accept files or downloads from people you don't personally know. (Yes—files and downloads are like the new candy from strangers that our parents told us to stay away from.)

Brain Games: Sharpening Your Mind with Puzzles & Trivia

It was mentioned earlier that brain teasers can be a fun and easy way to keep your mind sharp, **so below are a few fun apps that you may find addictive:**

- **Wordle:** A word puzzle game in which players try to guess a secret five-letter word within six attempts, receiving feedback on correct letters and their positions after each guess.

- **Lumosity:** Offers a collection of brain-training games designed to enhance cognitive skills like memory, attention, and problem solving through engaging and interactive challenges.

- **Online Chess:** This one's been around for decades, and it's a fun way to connect with other players from all over the world. You can even get an official rating while playing virtual games.

- **Elevate:** Focuses on improving communication and analytical skills by offering personalized daily challenges, including reading comprehension, writing, math, and more.

- **Peak:** Provides a variety of mini-games to challenge memory, attention, language, problem solving, and mental agility, helping users exercise different facets of their cognitive abilities.

- **Sudoku**: A classic number puzzle game that stimulates logical thinking and pattern recognition, requiring players to fill a 9 x 9 grid with digits from 1 to 9 without repetition in each row, column, and 3 x 3 subgrid. It's not as complicated as it sounds!

Whoa! The Best Virtual Reality Apps for Seniors

Virtual reality (or VR) can require pretty elaborate headwear that fully immerses you in the visual and audio aspects of the virtual world you're trying to enter. These headsets can cost a few hundred dollars (or more), but they're an exciting opportunity for people with a deep interest in VR.

If you'd like to get your toes wet without spending a fortune, there are cheaper headsets that utilize your phone screen to render VR worlds.

Here are some really great VR apps to consider:

- **NatureTreks VR:** This is a walking simulator that supplies players with serene environments to navigate and explore.

- **Real VR Fishing:** Available on the Meta Quest device, Real VR Fishing is a fishing simulator that allows players to explore their favorite hobby in a wide range of different settings. If you like the idea of deep-sea fishing but not enough to buy a plane ticket, this may be the next best thing.

- **Guided Tai Chi:** Exactly what it sounds like! This is a guided exercise app that allows you to explore the ancient art of Tai Chi with the help of an instructor on Quest devices.

- **Shores of Loci:** This immersive puzzle game is designed to stimulate the mind and excite the senses.

Volunteering Online: The World Is Only a Click Away

We *really* know that we're in the 21st century when we don't even have to leave our homes to volunteer to the causes we care about. The online world isn't just about finding entertainment opportunities—we can connect with almost anything that we're passionate about, including opportunities to donate our time and money to worthy causes.

Sometimes, this will mean connecting with in-person volunteer opportunities, and you can bet that volunteer organizations within your community will do the majority of their self-promotion online.

Other times, you'll find opportunities to volunteer remotely, helping real people from the comfort of your home.

Virtual Tutoring: Share Your Knowledge with the Next Generation

A couple of the mentoring opportunities described in the previous chapter operated strictly online, but there are also opportunities to teach people remotely. These volunteer opportunities are generally flexible and open to anyone who can verify a requisite level of competence in their subject area. In other words, you don't necessarily need to have been a teacher in your previous career to volunteer as a tutor online— you just need to show that you know your stuff.

The following are a few online tutoring opportunities worth checking out:

- **Paper**: An online platform that connects tutors with students who need help in various subjects. Tutors can volunteer their time to support students remotely.

- **UPchieve**: A non-profit organization that provides free, online tutoring to underserved high school students. Volunteers can sign up to tutor subjects like math, science, and language arts.

- **Wyzant**: While this is primarily a platform for paid tutoring, some tutors offer free sessions or volunteer their time. You can create a profile and indicate your willingness to volunteer.

- **TutorMate**: Focuses on providing virtual tutoring for elementary school students. Volunteers can help improve students' reading skills through online sessions.

Online Advocacy: Use Your Voice for a Cause

If you spend just five minutes on the internet, you'll quickly find that people love nothing more than to use it to share their opinions (sometimes to great excess and little effect). Still, targeted online advocacy is a great way to spotlight causes that are important to you.

For every person drowning the web in unsolicited political opinions, there are other, quieter social advocates calling attention to worthy causes.

Use your online platform as a way to draw attention to volunteer or donating opportunities. Spread awareness to underrecognized causes, and speak up to do some good.

Digital Creatives: Graphic Design, Writing & More

You can also provide services to non-profit organizations using your computer. If you're a capable writer, you could volunteer to handle social media captions, email copy, or fundraiser documents for an organization you care about.

If you're a talented artist, you could volunteer graphic design services. If you're handy with computers and tech (and reading this chapter out of the kindness of your heart), you could help with website administration.

Charity organizations operate on shoestring budgets and generally could use all the help they can get. Regardless of what your talent is, there are almost certainly ways that you can leverage it to support a cause you care about.

If you aren't sure how you can help, the best move is simply to reach out and ask. Chances are you'll get plenty of suggestions.

Finding Your Perfect Virtual Volunteer Opportunity

Most organizations have a pretty robust online presence at this point. In many cases, this also means that they'll have many ways in which you can provide support to them online. Below, we've listed out a few opportunities that you might want to consider. Keep in mind, however, that this list is *far* from comprehensive. There are more than one million non-profit organizations registered in the United States [16], and many of them will have virtual support volunteer opportunities.

- **Trevor Project:** An organization committed to helping youths struggling with coming out, thoughts of suicide, and other difficulties common for LGBTQ+ youths. You can volunteer as a crisis counselor after completing 40 hours of training.

- **United Nations:** The UN has a wide range of virtual support opportunities listed on its website. This can include everything from teaching and mentoring to project development.

- **Career Village:** An online resource for children who want to know more about the realities of various career paths. Helpful volunteers answer their questions via Career Village's platform.

- **Smithsonian Museum:** This world-renowned research and museum complex gives virtual volunteers the opportunity to transcribe and review various documents.

Key Takeaways

- Delving into the online world is easier than you might think. Smart devices are made to be generally accessible and there are lots of resources to help you along the way.

- The internet is a great way to connect with free entertainment in the form of podcasts and video content. Explore based on your interests, but try your best to be a discerning consumer. A lot of content is better than others, so always know your source.

- Video games aren't just for kids. There are plenty of fun games that can stimulate your brain and help you unwind at the end of the day.

- The internet is a fantastic place to find volunteer opportunities and lend your time to worthy causes and organizations.

Chapter 6

Born To Run: Traveling After 50

"To my mind, the greatest reward and luxury of travel is to be able to experience everyday things as if for the first time, to be in a position in which almost nothing is so familiar [that it's] taken for granted."
-Bill Bryson, author

Bill Bryson got it right when he described travel as a way of seeing the world anew. One of the nicest things about stepping out of the familiar is getting to discover new experiences. And by the time we reach our fifties, that's a rare opportunity.

Traveling can be a little overwhelming. The world is a big place, so where does one even begin? In this chapter, we'll take a look at notable locations and what you can do there.

Iconic Cities to Explore

Big cities are where all the big stuff happens. If you're interested in fine dining or the arts, you'll find that nothing compares to a large metropolitan area. While city traveling *does* have a way of eating away at your bank account—you might need to take out a small loan just to afford parking in certain areas—it's worthwhile for people who want to enjoy an energetic environment full of beauty, culture—and rats. Very, very large rats.

Below, we highlight some of the most notable cities on the planet.

The Big Apple: Must-Sees in NYC

It goes without saying that New York City is the melting pot of the United States and one of the most significant cultural hubs on the entire planet. Whether you're a lover of art and culture, fine dining, or simple sightseeing, there's truly something there for everyone. You'll *never* run out of things to see while you are there—which is super, because you likely won't want to spend too much time in your shoe-box-sized hotel room—unless you're a Rockefeller yourself and can spring for a lavish suite!

Below are a few of the many incredible attractions in New York City, **aside from the ones you likely already know like Central Park and Times Square:**

- **The Metropolitan Museum of Art:** "The Met" houses one of the most extensive and valuable art collections in the country. From ancient artifacts to modern masterpieces, immerse yourself in art, history, and culture.

- **Statue of Liberty and Ellis Island:** This is the sort of thing that you just *can't* skip. Even if you've never been to New York before, the Statue of Liberty is iconic enough to inspire a sense of moving nostalgia in almost anyone who sees it.

- **City Reliquary Museum:** This feast for the eyes provides a visual history of the city's five boroughs. It's a modest but very unique collection that includes stories about everything from New York sports franchises and gangsters to the tales of local bakeries.

And don't forget—New York is famous for its bagels and pizza. Don't worry about the carb overload—you'll definitely burn it off walking the streets.

City of Love: Romantic Paris

There's a reason that Paris is considered the city of romance—it's full of beauty, art, and fine dining. It's existed as a city since the third century (that's *not* a typo), which means that it's full of history and culture in a way that cities in a relatively young nation like the United States simply can't compete with.

Let's explore some of Paris' gems below before you make plans to explore them in person:

- **Louvre Museum:** Home to thousands of works, including the Mona Lisa and the Venus de Milo, this iconic museum is a can't-miss stop on your tour of Paris.

- **Eiffel Tower:** Can you imagine visiting this city and *not* visiting the Eiffel Tower? Think how your friends and family would scold you if you told them that you missed this bucket-list item. Fortunately, it's worth visiting for more than just the social pressure—it's a beautiful and iconic location that'll give you views of the entire city.

- **Montmartre and Sacré-Cœur Basilica:** You'll feel like you walked into the 18th century as you explore Montmartre's charming streets. Make sure to climb to the top of the hill to reach the Sacré-Cœur Basilica, offering panoramic views of Paris.

Keep in mind that Paris is also a major fashion capital of the world. If you're passionate about clothes or just want to take a look at what sort of shirt costs a month's mortgage payment, set aside some time to visit a few of the many boutiques around town. And while you're out, stop for a pastry or a macaron! Counting calories in Europe is a fool's errand!

La Dolce Vita: Rome's Ancient Wonders

Rome is over 2,700 years old, which means it predates Christianity by almost a millennium. The city has changed a lot in that time, but there are still plenty of old monuments and landmarks to take in. The oldest building in Rome is the Pantheon, which also has the distinction of being the oldest recognized building *on the planet*.

Below are some unforgettable things to do "when in Rome":

- **Colosseum:** While it's been centuries since the Colosseum last hosted a tournament, the iconic building still carries significant historical weight.

- **Roman Forum:** Ages ago, the Roman Forum was the very center of social and political life. While that's no longer the case, there are still plenty of fascinating sights to take in at this ancient and historic location.

- **Vatican City and St. Peter's Basilica:** While you're in the area, be sure to take a trip to Vatican City, the smallest independent state in the world, and visit St. Peter's Basilica. You don't have to be Catholic or even Christian to appreciate the history and architectural beauty.

- **The Spanish Steps:** Tackle a steep incline that leads up to the Trinita dei Monti church. The Steps were an engineering marvel when they were first built in the early 1700s. Today they remain a beautiful and culturally enriching way to keep your Fitbit happy.

Be sure to eat your heart out while you are there! Rome is, of course, well-known for its pizza and pasta, but while you're there, also try eating as the locals do. Fresh, locally sourced ingredients are a major staple of authentic Italian cuisine.

The Land Down Under: Sydney's Vibrance

It's often joked that Australia is full of animals that can—and quite possibly will—kill you. In fact, there's a high concentration of critters with sharp teeth and more than your average amount of poison. The good news? The views and experiences in Sydney Australia are actually to die for, so the risk will be worth it.

Sydney combines a major metropolitan area with beautiful beaches, making it a great place to experience the cultural opportunities of a big city while allowing you plenty of opportunities to enjoy nature.

A list of some fabulous things to do in Sydney:

- **Sydney Opera House:** This world-renowned architectural masterpiece is situated on the stunning Sydney Harbor. Whether attending a performance or simply enjoying the views, the iconic symbol of Sydney is a must-see.

- **Bondi Beach:** Soak up the sun at one of Sydney's most famous stretches of sand. Just watch out for sharks and jellyfish. Seriously—they're everywhere.

- **Taronga Zoo:** While it may seem a little silly to cross the planet and wind up at a zoo, this one may just be worth your time. Taronga is world-renowned for hosting one of the largest collections of animals on the planet.

Seafood lovers rejoice! Sydney is also well-known for capitalizing on its coastal position to deliver some of the best fish dishes on the planet.

Affordable City Adventures

If you're overwhelmed by the idea of visiting a city that requires you to cross an ocean, there are countless fascinating and affordable cities in the United States to consider. They don't even need to be the biggest cities in the country—beauty and culture are found all over this great nation of ours.

Below, we'll examine a few worthwhile cities to visit that won't break your budget:

- **St. Louis:** While St. Louis is known to many people as simply being home to the Gateway Arch, it's actually a vibrant and affordable city with plenty to do. Love sports? Consider catching a Blues, Cardinals, or STL City game. Enjoy fine dining? Stop over at iconic neighborhood The Hill for an authentic Italian dining experience. St. Louis is also well-known for its wide range of free museums and attractions, including its zoo—which just happens to be one of the highest-rated in the country.

- **Chicago:** While Chicago can get a little pricey, it's much cheaper and more accessible than New York while offering a comparable(ish) range of attractions. From Navy Pier to Sears Tower (now known as Willis Tower—not that anyone calls it that), there are plenty of landmarks to take in. It's also famous for great pizza, exquisite shopping, and several major sports franchises.

- **Memphis:** Well known for its vibrant music culture, this city is a frequent pilgrimage destination for fans of rock and roll, so be sure to stop by Graceland before hitting Beale Street for a fun night on the town. Tuck into a pulled pork sandwich while you're there—the city is famous for them!

This list is *far* from comprehensive—there are dozens of affordable cities in the United States just waiting to be explored. When calculating the price of a city adventure, there are, of course, several factors to consider. The price of the hotel rooms available can certainly indicate overall financial accessibility, but also think about how much the attractions will cost. Are there affordable restaurants? Will you need to fly or can you drive? These factors may ultimately play a bigger part in determining the total cost of your trip.

Take Me Home, Country Roads: Unforgettable Rural Retreats

Cities are a great way to enjoy an action-packed adventure, but sometimes it's nice to slow down and enjoy a more relaxed, rural pace of life. The world is full of beautiful country retreats, so let's look at some notable locations to explore below.

Tuscan Sun: Italy's Rustic Charm

You'll often hear the phrase "rolling hills" mentioned in the same breath as the word "Tuscany." This region of Italy is famous for its vineyards and olive groves. It produces some of—if not the very greatest—olive oil in the entire world, and it's famous for hearty, flavorful pasta composed of locally sourced ingredients.

It's also near the Leaning Tower of Pisa, as well as several notable museums and art galleries that'll appeal to those looking for a more cultural experience. **The following are some things to keep on your radar:**

- **Wine Tasting in Chianti:** Explore the picturesque Chianti region, known for—you guessed it—delicious Chianti wine. Fancy a fancy tipple?

- **Visit Florence's Uffizi Gallery:** Marvel at masterpieces by Michelangelo, Leonardo da Vinci, and Botticelli in the Uffizi Gallery, located in the heart of Florence.

When eating in Tuscany, don't forget to ask your waiter (in whatever broken Italian you can manage) for their recommendation. Because Tuscan cuisine is so dependent on the quality of the ingredients, the "best dish to eat" will depend on what time of year you go. Fresh produce for the win!

Highland Haven: Scotland's Stunning Scenery

The Scottish Highlands look very much like a land from a different era. If you've ever wanted to step into a fantasy novel, this may be the next best thing. The region is full of beautiful natural locations but also brilliant castles and other historical buildings that are great fun to explore.

Below are some things to do in the Scottish Highlands:

- **Loch Ness Cruise and Monster Hunt:** Embark on a cruise across the storied Loch Ness, absorbing the stunning scenery while keeping an eye out for the legendary Nessie.

- **Whisky Tasting at a Highland Distillery:** Indulge in the rich flavors of Scotch whisky by visiting a traditional Highland distillery. They say that it tastes better here than anywhere else.

The Scottish Highlands aren't known for their culinary treats in the same way that Italy is. Haggis is perhaps the most notable flavor of the region—a dish made from minced organ meats. And you know the old saying: "When in Rome, do as the Romans do." So when in Scotland, eat a sheep's heart.

Outback Odyssey: Australia's Untamed Wilderness

Earlier it was mentioned that Australia is known for its dangerous animals. Well, the outback is where those animals live. It's not a singular location but rather a massive, primarily undeveloped region of the country that accounts for about 80% of the continent's land mass. And that's a *lot* of land mass.

The following are a couple of suggestions for where to start your adventure:

- **Uluru-Kata Tjuta National Park (North):** Explore the sacred monolith of Uluru and the impressive rock formations of Kata Tjuta, delving into the spiritual and natural wonders of the Red Centre.

- **Flinders Ranges (South):** Discover the breathtaking landscapes of the Flinders Ranges, featuring deep gorges, red rock formations, and ancient Aboriginal cultural sites.

Note that significant preparation is recommended before you set out on an outback adventure. Don't let the steakhouse chain mislead you—it can be rough out there. Find guides who can help make your trip safer, and begin conditioning (and bracing yourself) at home.

Budget-Friendly Rural Getaways

Naturally, you don't need to leave the country to enjoy a rural adventure. The United States is full of small towns and vibrant farm land to explore. While these parts of the country are often overlooked, they're home to some really exciting—and often affordable—travel opportunities.

Below are just a few of the many opportunities you might want to explore on the domestic front.

- **Fredericksburg, Texas:** Explore this charming, German-influenced town with its historic Main Street, lined with boutique shops, art galleries, and local eateries. There are vineyards nearby, and plenty of small town charm to enjoy. You can grab a frozen sangria and walk the streets, too—it's legal there!

- **Eureka Springs, Arkansas:** Wander through the Victorian-style streets of Eureka Springs, known for its preserved 19th-century architecture. The town is a pleasant blend of quirks, art, history, and charm.

- **Stowe, Vermont:** The state of Vermont has been quaint and charming since well before Bernie Sanders put on those mittens (if you don't get the reference from Biden's inauguration in January 2021, there are plenty of memes online—check them out on your smartphone with the tips from last chapter!). While there are almost endless pleasant locations to explore, Stowe is particularly noted for its scenic views and small-town fun.

To be honest, every single region of the United States will have comparable options to the ones listed above. Guaranteed, there are interesting and lively rural communities within fifty miles of every major city in the United States, so do a little bit of research and set out for an exciting exploration of your local area.

Exotic Destinations & Local Gems

Cities and rural exploration are great, but sometimes it's important to step out of your comfort zone a little and see things that you just won't find in the Western world. Coming up, we'll explore truly exotic locations that may just change the way you see the world.

And if you're on a budget? We'll also look at ways in which you can enjoy an exotic experience in your own backyard.

Land of the Rising Sun: Japan's Cultural Gems

Japan is idealized by many Americans for great reason. The country is famous for blending spirituality and art into every aspect of its culture— from architecture to basic cultural practices. While Japan has a diverse landscape similar to most countries of its size, we've summarized just a handful of incredible things you won't want to miss in the Land of the Rising Sun.

- **Tokyo's Tsukiji Fish Market:** Explore the bustling market, savoring fresh sushi and seafood delicacies in one of the biggest fish markets on the planet. It's the sort of thing you didn't even know you wanted to see!

- **Hiroshima Peace Memorial Park:** This is a touching monument to the victims of the atomic bomb. While thinking about the many innocent victims of World War II isn't everyone's idea of vacation fun, it *is* an important way to honor and learn from the lives lost in one of human history's great tragedies.

- **Mount Fuji's Chureito Pagoda:** Capture breathtaking views of Mount Fuji from the Chureito Pagoda, an iconic spot offering a stunning panorama of the mountain and cherry blossoms. While you're there, see if you can find out where they bottle all of that really expensive water with the same name.

- **Hakone's Onsen Experience:** After all your sightseeing, cherry-blossom smelling, and seafood indulging, relax in Hakone's hot springs surrounded by beautiful views. You've earned it.

- **Kyoto:** No longer the capital city of Japan, the city still remains a beautiful hub of cultural spirituality. Take in the Buddhist shrines and enjoy some fine dining as you explore fascinating Kyoto.

Japan is well-known for a fairly wide range of different culinary options. Fish plays a particularly big role in most Japanese diets, so be sure to enjoy some fresh catches while you're there.

African Adventure: Safari Excursions & More

Traveling to Africa is an admittedly enormous undertaking. Not only is the plane ride wildly long but you may also need to speak with your doctor about what precautions to take before your trip. The risk of malaria and other mosquito borne illnesses is very real there.

Spook stories aside, the truth is that you shouldn't let the risks and necessary precautions deter you. With proper planning, you can enjoy a safe trip to Africa—and it'll be well-worth your time to do so. **Below are some reasons why:**

- **Safari in the Serengeti or Maasai Mara (Tanzania/Kenya):** These regions are famous for hosting some of the most beautiful and rare animals on the planet. It's a great place to respectfully explore nature in a way that simply isn't possible anywhere else.

- **Victoria Falls (Zambia/Zimbabwe):** If you thought that the people of Niagara have it good, wait until you see Victoria Falls. Marvel at this must-see waterfall, which just happens to be one of the largest on the planet.

- **Cape Town and Table Mountain (South Africa):** Africa isn't all about safariing. While you're there, explore exciting Cape Town and get a taste of the local culture.

- **Cultural Exploration in Marrakech (Morocco):** Immerse yourself in the vibrant colors, flavors, and traditions of this fascinating nation that's famous for its colorful architecture and bustling marketplaces.

While people typically imagine great plains and safari experiences when they think about Africa, it's important to keep in mind that we're actually talking about an *entire* continent. There are 54 countries—all of which are culturally distinct [17]. In fact, Africa is the second largest continent on the planet.

In other words, there's no shortage of different kinds of experiences you can have there. You just need to plan accordingly.

Mystic East: Thailand's Temples & Beaches

Thailand is known for its beautiful Buddhist temples, lush jungles, and breathtaking beaches. Whether you're looking for a rich cultural experience in Bangkok or a more spiritual awakening in one of the many temples, **there are many ways to experience this beautiful and unique country:**

- **Island Hopping in the Andaman Sea (e.g., Phuket, Krabi):** Explore the stunning beaches, limestone cliffs, and vibrant marine life by hopping between the picturesque islands in the Andaman Sea.

- **Visit the Grand Palace and Wat Pho in Bangkok:** Experience the rich cultural heritage of Thailand by exploring the opulent Grand Palace and the iconic reclining Buddha at Wat Pho in the bustling city of Bangkok.

- **Floating Markets in Damnoen Saduak and Amphawa:** Immerse yourself in the vibrant atmosphere of Thailand's floating markets, where you can shop for local goods and indulge in delicious street food. And yes, the word "floating" is used literally—goods are sold off the riverfront from small boats, providing a unique experience you won't find anywhere else.

Fun fact: Thailand is only one of several nations in the world to have Buddhism as its primary religion [18]. Western visitors with limited exposure to Eastern religions are often delighted and amazed by what they learn about Buddhist traditions.

Staying Frugal in Faraway Places

International travel often feels a little more inaccessible than it really is. You start thinking about how far from home you'll be, and all you see is money leaving your pocket. The truth is that international travel doesn't have to cost all that much more than domestic trips.

The main difference will usually be the flight. For one thing, unless you're going to Canada or Mexico (or you have a really interesting automobile that we haven't heard about), driving won't be an option.

And overseas flights typically cost more than their domestic alternatives

But you can make them more affordable by:

- **Timing Your Trips Well:** You can often save a lot of money on plane tickets by buying them well in advance. Some experts even recommend buying your tickets about six months before the flight [19]. Tickets are usually at their most expensive the moment they're announced—which can be as much as a year in advance for some flights. The price slowly trickles down to reflect demand, only to increase again as you near the date in question.

- **Using Points.** You can receive great discounts on plane tickets and hotel rooms by using credit card points with that particular reward incentive attached. Look for cards with big spend bonuses and rewards partnerships—just be sure to pay the cards off each month so that you don't rack up consumer debt (and travel can be a *very* easy way to do this).

- **Picking Your Hotels Wisely.** If you want to book an affordable trip to NYC, don't look for hotel rooms in Manhattan. It's sometimes harder to have that same rationale in an international city, but similar rules apply. If you don't want to pay city rates, look for cheaper options within a thirty-mile radius of the place you want to spend most of your time. You may be surprised by how much the room rates drop.

- **Considering Airbnb.** This platform is great because the rooms often come with their own kitchens, and that's generally a given if you're booking full apartments. This can help you save money on dining out. While you do want to try the local cuisine while you're exploring an international city, eating out three times a day every day can add up fast.

There are always ways to receive a discount if you give yourself enough time to properly research your options. Spend some time online and find out what makes the most sense for you. Time is always your friend when it comes to planning a big trip. The more room you have to figure out the details, the easier it'll be to find cost-effective ways to accomplish what you want.

Cultural Events, Excursions & Festivals in Your Own Backyard

You don't have to have an international budget to enjoy an international experience. Many communities host international festivals, in which people from all over the world gather to share their food, music, and cultural artifacts.

These festivals aren't quite the same as standing in an ancient Buddhist temple, but they can be invigorating and educational just the same. You can even make a trip out of it—research international festivals within a one-hundred-mile radius and plan an exciting weekend excursion!

Come Sail Away: Cruises & Boat Trips

Ahoy! Cruises and boat trips are a beautiful way to experience travel in a relaxed and leisurely environment. The old saying, "Life's a journey—not a destination" is the mindset behind most cruises and boat trips, and the journey is generally guaranteed to be stunning.

Below, we'll take a look at an overview of traveling by sea. Be prepared for clear skies, smooth waters, and…scurvy? Nothing a nice brunch mimosa can't cure!

Cruising for Novices

Cruising is a little bit different from traditional modes of travel. If you've never done it, you likely won't have a very good idea of what you are getting yourself into. **Here's a breakdown of some cruise fast facts that might help you enjoy the experience more thoroughly:**

- Cruises are a great way to see lots of different places. They usually stop at port cities, giving passengers the opportunity to get out and explore a little. If you'd like to scratch a bunch of places off your travel bucket list in one go, this is an efficient way to do it.

- They're also great for solo travelers. Cruise ships tend to be more social than hotels because everyone is stuck (although that word tends not to appear on many cruise ship brochures) in the same confined space, though it's likely more vast than you can even imagine. There are plenty of activities and social opportunities that single travelers can comfortably experience on their own.

- They can be surprisingly economical—many cruise ships offer food and drinks included in your base rate. This gives more expenditure transparency than you'll find in many other types of trips.

That said, they aren't perfect. Not everyone responds well to choppy waters. Your room will almost certainly be quite small. And you may even feel a little stir-crazy if given enough time at sea. Still, cruising remains a favorite pastime for thousands of people all over the world, so these cruise lines are most definitely doing something right!

Island Hopping in the Caribbean

The Caribbean is a relatively large oceanic region known for its blue seas and delightfully tropical islands. Notable locations include Cuba, Jamaica, Puerto Rico, and North Andros. Caribbean cruise lines are fairly common, so you should have no shortage of options to explore.

Mediterranean Magic: Europe's Coastal Delights

The Mediterranean includes Greece, Italy, San Pietro, Crete, and so many of Europe's other most picturesque coastal destinations. The region's diet—which consists of fish, vegetables, and healthy fats—is widely celebrated as the healthiest cuisine on the planet. In other words, this will be what doctors call a "medicinal cruise." Bottoms up to that!

Exploring the World's Great Rivers & Waterways

Little known fact: Cruises don't have to be exotic, and they don't even have to take place on the ocean. The United States is home to some massive rivers and waterways, many of which have a decent cruise scene. For example, there are cruise lines that travel the Mighty Mississippi— some of which have more than 20 stops along the 2000-plus miles of river.

Or maybe you're passionate about the Great Lakes region and its mysterious black squirrels. If that sounds like you, why not spend two weeks exploring five of the largest freshwater sources on the planet?

If there's a large body of water that you're interested in, chances are someone has figured out how to design a cruise around it.

Budget-Friendly Cruising Tips

You can enjoy cruises at a wide range of different price points. **Below are a few tips that might be helpful to keep in mind as you book your next aquatic adventure:**

- Opt for off-peak seasons or last-minute bookings to take advantage of discounted cruise prices.

- Consider interior cabins or lower-tier staterooms, as they're often more budget-friendly than suites with ocean views.

- Research and compare different cruise lines, looking for promotions, package deals, and inclusive amenities to find the best value for your budget.

Keep in mind that there may also be shorter excursions within your area. Even day cruises down large rivers or big lakes can be a fun way to unwind, so find out what opportunities are available near you.

Baby, You Can Drive My Car: Road Trips

Car journeys tend to be an affordable way to see the country at your own pace. Sure, you'll spend a lot of time behind the wheel, but now that you've learned all about the huge variety of podcasts out there, that won't feel like such a big deal anymore.

Let's explore a few interesting road trip ideas. However, the really nice thing about setting off for the open road in your car is that the experience is very flexible. Feel free to take our suggestions, or throw caution to the wind and set off with nothing more than a great Spotify playlist and a head full of dreams.

Route 66: America's Main Street

Route 66 was one of the first original major highways in the United States. At its inception, it was designed to let drivers go all the way from Chicago to California without ever needing to change highways. It's been changed and reconfigured since then, and so it's no longer the marvel of engineering that it once was.

Still, it's definitely worth exploring for road trip enthusiasts. **The following are a few unbeatable stops to consider:**

- The iconic Cadillac Ranch in Amarillo, Texas features a lineup of colorful, graffiti-covered vintage Cadillacs buried nose-down into the ground, creating a unique roadside art installation.

- The Grand Canyon Caverns in Arizona offer an unparalleled underground adventure. With guided tours showcasing stunning limestone formations and a cavern so large it can house multiple football fields, you'll be positively awestruck. You can even spend the night in a surprisingly comfortable hotel room built right into the cavern (though it'll set you back about $1000 or more per night).

- The historic Wigwam Motel in Holbrook, Arizona presents a nostalgic experience with its distinctive teepee-shaped accommodations, providing a glimpse into the quirky charm of Route 66's motels.

While you're on the road, you'll quickly see that there are countless other attractions built along the highway. Stop at whatever catches your eye, but be aware that attractions advertising "the real Bigfoot" likely haven't been scientifically vetted.

Cali's Pacific Coast: Highway 1 Wonders

The California Pacific Coast Highway, also known as Highway 1, is a scenic and iconic highway that runs along the coastline of the golden state. It stretches for about 655 miles from the southern part of California near Dana Point in Orange County to Leggett in Mendocino County in the north.

The highway offers breathtaking views of the Pacific Ocean, coastal cliffs, rugged landscapes, and various landmarks. If you're already making an extended stay in California, it's a fun way to leisurely spend two or three days exploring one of the most famous, and certainly most attractive, highways in the United States.

Make plenty of stops along the way. Like any good highway, there are plenty of interesting things just waiting for people willing to pull over for a while.

The Great Ocean Road: Australia's Scenic Drive

It would be crazy to go to Australia *just* for a drive. But if you do find yourself in the land down under, why not spend a little bit of time on one of the most beautiful highways on the planet? This Australian National Heritage listed site treats drivers to more than a hundred miles of ocean views. It's an easy day trip with countless great views. There are also lots of interesting stops along the way, including Port Cambell and Apollo Bay. If you want to explore Australia thoroughly but don't know where to start, this could be your answer.

Romantic Road: Germany's Historic Route

It really *is* a romantic road. Germany's historic highway route cuts through old-fashioned German towns, rolling hills, and heavily forested areas offering a picturesque tour of the country. Make sure to set aside plenty of time to explore all the cute little German towns (with big, complicated German names).

Finding Your Own Local Scenic Drives & Attractions

You don't have to go to Australia or Germany to go on a jaw-dropping drive. The American highway system is full of scenic areas. Conduct a little bit of research and find out what notable stops are available in your area. Highway attractions aren't as prominent as they once were, but there are still plenty of wonderful things to see just off the highway.

Plus, can you really consider your life complete if you've never laid eyes on the world's biggest ball of twine? (Now that we've intrigued you, it's in Cawker City, Kansas.)

Life Is a Highway: The RV Lifestyle in Retirement

If you go to any RV park in the country, you'll find that the age demographic shifts decidedly in the direction of "retired—or pretty close to it." There are certainly families that head out for shared camping experiences in an RV, but the camper lifestyle appeals naturally to retired people who want to travel comfortably at an affordable price.

While the sticker price for the RV itself is usually high, booking a reservation at a campsite will generally be very cheap. This makes it easy to go anywhere, anytime without worrying about the sometimes prohibitive prices of dining out or staying in a hotel.

RV Travel Basics for Beginners

While RV living isn't exactly difficult, it does require a little more thoughtfulness than you're required to exercise in houses that don't have wheels. For one thing, it's important to keep in mind that RVs straddle two sides of a fairly expensive dividing line—they're both homes and cars and require upkeep in *both* departments.

The housing aspect is generally financially manageable—even large RVs are small enough to be cleaned and maintained with relative ease by the average person. You may have the occasional plumbing or electric issue to contend with, but for the most part, it's pretty accessible maintenance.

The automotive aspect can be more expensive. Some people put the annual cost of ownership at around 10% of the RVs sticker price, but that's not necessarily accurate.

Here's what'll actually happen: You'll have some years during which maintenance costs are negligible, and other years when you're hit with several huge repairs in a row. In other words—it's a car. A huge, house car.

Another thing to bear in mind is that getting electricity and water is solely on you, and you'll have to attach hookups at your site every night. It can be a bit of a hassle after ten hours on the road to set your RV up—although the actual time it takes to do everything right isn't overly demanding once you get in the habit.

Here's the big thing—waste management. What goes into the RV toilet has to go out somewhere else. Draining the sewage tank isn't a fun job, but someone has to do it. (And that someone will be you.)

While these pain points aren't very appealing, those who can accept them are rewarded with a lifestyle entirely centered around travel and freedom.

Top RV Adventure Ideas for Retirees

The United States highway system includes hundreds of thousands of miles of paved roads, so there are literally endless opportunities to explore the country in an RV. No list could possibly reflect the full scope of opportunities to sightsee in an RV, **including ours featured below, but it's a solid starting point:**

- **Route 66 Expedition:** Take a nostalgic journey along the historic Route 66, spanning from Chicago to Santa Monica. Use our earlier mentions of Route 66 for exploration ideas, but keep in mind that there are so many more things to do on that historic highway than anyone could possibly mention.

- **Blue Ridge Parkway Exploration:** Traverse the scenic Blue Ridge Parkway, renowned for its stunning views of the

Appalachian Highlands. This leisurely drive takes you through lush forests, rolling hills, and charming Appalachian communities.

- **Desert Southwest Adventure:** Tour the captivating desert landscapes of the American Southwest. Visit places like Sedona, Grand Canyon, Joshua Tree National Park, and Monument Valley. The region offers a blend of unique geological formations, vibrant sunsets, and opportunities for stargazing.

- **Great Lakes Discovery:** Explore the beauty of the Great Lakes region, with visits to places like Mackinac Island (you can't bring your RV there, but you can get out and take the ferry), Door County, and the Apostle Islands. Enjoy the scenic shorelines, lighthouses, and freshwater landscapes. You may be surprised by how significantly varied the communities along the Great Lakes are. From small-town America to Canada's greatest city of Toronto, there's no shortage of incredible places to explore.

- Pro tip? You can get a fairly decent rental rate on RVs. Consider leasing one for a month and seeing how you like it before you commit to ownership.

Pros & Cons of RV Living

Below, we break down the most salient points for deciding if RV living is right for you.

Pros:

- **Mobility and Flexibility:** RV living provides the freedom to travel and explore different locations. You can change your scenery regularly, visit new places, and experience different cultures, departing for new locations any time the mood hits you.

- **Cost Savings:** Living in an RV can absolutely be more cost-effective than traditional housing. RV owners save money on rent or mortgage payments, property taxes, and utility bills. Additionally, you have the option to cook your own meals, reducing your dining out expenses.

- **Connection with Nature:** RV living often allows you to immerse yourself in natural surroundings. Whether parked in a campground, near a beach, or in the mountains, you can enjoy the beauty of nature—and it's always right at your doorstep.

- **Community:** RV parks and campgrounds often host a vibrant community of fellow RVers. This provides opportunities to connect with like-minded individuals, share experiences, and build lasting friendships on the road. You may be surprised how often road warriors wind up congregating at the same locations.

Cons:

- **Limited Space:** One of the main challenges of RV living is the limited living quarters. It requires careful organization and downsizing, which can be difficult for those accustomed to larger, more traditional homes.

- **Maintenance and Repairs:** RVs require regular maintenance, and breakdowns can happen unexpectedly. Repairing or maintaining an RV can be more challenging and costly than fixing issues in a traditional home, especially if you're not mechanically inclined.

- **Lack of Stability:** Living in an RV means a constantly changing environment, which may not be suitable for everyone. The lack of a permanent home can lead to a sense of instability, making it challenging for individuals who thrive on routine and consistency.

Keep in mind that some of these cons aren't relevant if you decide to also maintain a stationary home (also known as a "house").

Creating a Budget for Your RV Adventures

A basic RV will cost anywhere from $20k to $100k (depending mostly on just how "basic" you're willing to go). Luxury RVs can cost millions of dollars, but you likely aren't in the market for one of those. Trailers, which are like RVs that get towed behind your car, usually cost a little less but they can be a little harder to haul and manage (as well as live in).

You also need to factor the cost of maintenance into your budget. While we scoffed at the "10% annual upkeep" figure from earlier, it may be a good reference point to use for planning purposes.

The cost of the RV itself is the most significant expense. From there, you can usually find affordable camping opportunities that fit almost any budget. Basic campsites may cost as little as $10 to $20 per night! More elaborate sites with high-quality bathhouses and amenities might cost closer to $100 per night, but you can pick and choose when you'd like to "splurge" on those.

Food expenses are also incredibly flexible. You can dine-in using the kitchenette in your RV or indulge from time to time in local cuisine— and most RV owners do a combination of both. You can even splurge and eat-in at the same time—there's nothing like a fire-grilled rib eye and shrimp skewers on your very own hibachi under the open skies.

Key Takeaways

- Whether you're flying, driving, or sailing, there are endless ways to explore the world.

- While travel is great for those with wanderlust, it's very possible to have a rewarding, multicultural experience right at home. Find out what intriguing stops are available in your community.

- Time is your friend. The earlier you plan your trips, the easier it'll be to find affordable accommodations.

- Budget traveling is all about controlling the priciest variables. Look for lodging accommodations that allow you to cook at home. Also, you can visit big cities but stay in more affordable surrounding towns to save on expenses.

Chapter 7

Ticket to Paradise: Relocation & Snowbird Hotspots

"If we were meant to stay in one place, we would have roots instead of feet."

-Rachel Wolchin, author

Rachel Wolchin's quote may not possess a scientific understanding of how roots are formed, but it does speak to a greater truth on the joys of stepping out of your comfort zone. Many people choose to relocate during retirement because they want to give a more favorable climate a try, or perhaps because they want to move closer to friends and family.

Whatever your motivation, there are countless appealing retiree-friendly destinations to consider. In this chapter, we'll take a look at some of the most interesting relocation and snowbird hotspots.

Today's Hottest Surprising US Retirement Destinations

Florida used to be the retirement cliché: Move there and spend the rest of your life forgetting about winter. While Florida does remain one of the most popular states in the country for people relocating from all over the world, it's no longer the undisputed champ. Below, we'll explore a few surprising retirement destinations that you might not have considered before.

Pacific Northwest Gems

The Pacific Northwest is well-known for its natural beauty, which is perhaps one of the factors that continues to attract retirees to the region in droves. It also boasts a mild climate and—in certain locations (specifically those not named "Portland")—the cost of living is fairly low.

Below are some satisfying spots in the Pacific Northwest to consider:

- **Bend, Oregon:** Nestled in the high desert, Bend offers an active lifestyle with world-class outdoor activities, a vibrant arts scene, and a friendly atmosphere, making it an ideal retirement destination.

- **Port Townsend, Washington:** This area's charming Victorian seaport, artistic community, and stunning waterfront views provide retirees with a tranquil yet engaging retirement locale with easy access to the mountains.

- **Ashland, Oregon:** Famed for the Oregon Shakespeare Festival, Ashland combines cultural richness, a mild climate, and a welcoming community, creating an enriching retirement experience.

- **Boise, Idaho:** A medium-sized city in the Pacific Northwest, Boise boasts something for everyone From art and history museums to a popular zoo, there are a plethora of fun city amenities to enjoy. It's also well known for its natural beauty, surrounded by gorgeous mountains and hiking excursion opportunities.

- **Eugene, Oregon:** This gorgeous spot in the Beaver State is known for its vibrant cultural scene and many greenspaces, which give Eugene a unique blend of culture and naturalism that's hard to find elsewhere.

- **Spokane, Washington:** Fittingly located along the Spokane River, this exciting city provides retirees with a balance of urban amenities, natural beauty, and an affordable cost of living for an enjoyable and fulfilling retirement.

Toledo, Ohio: A Midwestern Surprise

The Midwest is sometimes called flyover country—people living closer to the coast see it mostly as the flat green dot they pass over in their airplanes while traveling to more suitable locations. Well, let those folks sleep on the Midwest then. It leaves more for the rest of us.

Enter Toledo, Ohio. A recent survey found that this small city was the most affordable place in the entire country to retire. Got your attention yet?

At the time of writing, it costs retirees only $37k a year to live in Toledo, which is about 20% less than the national average [20]. Toledo also is fairly good looking. It's close to Lake Eerie, has a decent art scene, is located within an hour of several really great hospitals, and its median house price is one-third the national average.

Chattanooga, Tennessee: Access to the Great Outdoors

Southern Living Magazine recently named Chattanooga the best place in the country to retire. Here's why: Chattanooga has four mild seasons, a low cost of living, favorable tax rates, and several attractive attractions, including a well-known aquarium and the Creative Discovery Museum (which *Southern Living* described as a "grandkid magnet").

It's also located near the beautiful Lookout Mountain, which has several notable areas, including Ruby Falls and Incline Railway.

Charleston, South Carolina: Coastal Civility

Charleston is popular with retirees because it boasts a subtropical climate with relatively mild, stormy seasons. The weather is consistently warm without being stifling, and while tropical storms *do* arise from time to time, they tend to be much less severe than the ones Florida is often embattled with.

It's also located within close driving distance of many excellent hospitals, and it has a well-developed retirement community just waiting for you to join.

Sunny Florida: Wish You Were Here

Hey, Florida is still high on our list. As mentioned earlier, it's one of the most popular locations in the entire country for people moving from a different state, and for good reason. Taxes are low, the weather is sublime, and there's a well-established retiree community that'll give you lots of peer-aged people to interact with.

Some great Sunshine State spots to consider:

- **Naples:** Renowned for its upscale amenities, Gulf Coast beaches, and abundant golf courses, Naples attracts retirees seeking a luxurious yet relaxed lifestyle with a plethora of cultural activities.

- **Sarasota:** Situated along the Gulf of Mexico, Sarasota offers retirees a blend of beautiful beaches, a vibrant arts scene, and a diverse culinary landscape, making it an appealing destination for those desiring cultural enrichment.

- **The Villages:** A sprawling active adult community, The Villages caters to retirees with its golf courses, recreational facilities, and numerous social activities, providing a dynamic and engaging retirement experience.

Carolina on My Mind: Raleigh, Durham & Asheville

We can't forget about North Carolina. Raleigh, Durham, and Asheville are three of the most popular places for retirees because they enjoy the same tropical climate as South Carolina, and they include a few extra benefits as well.

For example, people aged 65 and up are allowed to audit (attend without credit) college courses for free in the state of North Carolina. The state has a lower cost of living than many coastal communities (this has made it a particularly popular destination for people moving from the more expensive Northeastern part of the country) and it is one of the top destinations in the country for baby chasers. And for those who don't know, the term doesn't describe deranged criminals but rather people who move across the country to live closer to their grown children.

Myrtle Beach: The Seaside Haven

Myrtle Beach is prized as a retirement location, one reason being because it's surprisingly affordable—the town has very carefully structured its tax incentives to attract retirees. These include a $15,000 annual tax deduction for people 65 and older, a "Homestead Exemption" that gives seniors a break on the first $50,000 of the property tax value, and more.

It's also a community structured around relaxation. Myrtle Beach boasts a number of award-winning golf courses, spas, and beaches, and it's conveniently located near scores of great restaurants. If you'd like your retired life to be as vacation-like as possible, Myrtle Beach is a great place to consider.

Rocky Mountain High: The Great Outdoors in Colorado

Colorado has the perfect combination of high culture (pun intended?) and natural beauty. It offers beautiful cities, a vibrant art scene, and lots of attractions to keep a retired person occupied, but it also has more hiking trails, skiing opportunities, and natural excursions than a person could really ever know what to do with. Below, we explore a few compelling retirement opportunities in Colorado.

Colorado Springs: Nature at Its Best

Colorado is ranked the eighth healthiest place to live in the entire nation [21]. It earned this designation by boasting clean mountain air and countless healthy outdoor recreational activities to choose from.

Whether you want to walk among the Garden of Gods (watch out for snakes—and yes, that's an Old Testament joke) or hike Rocky Mountain National Park, there are endless opportunities for outdoor exploration.

Colorado also allows a $24,000 deduction in taxable income for people aged 65 and over, making it an affordable place to lay down roots in your twilight years.

Affordable Outdoor Adventures in Colorado

While many people associate Colorado with skiing—which is decidedly not free—**it actually has an amazing number of low-cost adventures available to people who love the great outdoors:**

- **Bike the Colorado Trail:** Experience the beauty of Colorado's wilderness by biking a section of the Colorado Trail. This long-distance route spans over 500 miles through the Rocky Mountains, offering breathtaking scenery and diverse terrain. Many sections of the trail are accessible for day trips or overnight backpacking adventures, providing an affordable way to explore the state's stunning landscapes. While parts of the trail are challenging, it should be approachable for people of moderate skill.

- **Backpacking in the Indian Peaks Wilderness:** Embark on a backpacking adventure in the Indian Peaks Wilderness, located near beautiful Boulder. This wilderness area features over 130 miles of trails, winding through pristine alpine lakes, lush forests, and rugged mountain terrain.

- **Explore Great Sand Dunes National Park:** Discover the otherworldly landscapes of Great Sand Dunes National Park and Preserve. Camping in the park's designated campgrounds or nearby national forest lands offers an affordable overnight option for those looking to extend their visit.

And if you're thinking, "Well, that's all nice, but I'm probably going to want to step inside every now and then," you most certainly can. Colorado also has an extremely vibrant art scene—many galleries and installations in Denver are free or feature affordable entry (particularly for senior citizens).

Below are some unforgettable opportunities to enjoy art and culture that you won't want to miss:

- **Street Art Tour in Denver**: Take a self-guided tour of the city's vibrant street art scene, exploring colorful murals, graffiti, and public art installations throughout its neighborhoods. If you check online, you'll find that there are "semi-guided" tours that may provide context for some of the street art and murals.

- **First Friday Art Walks**: These monthly events in various Colorado cities—including Denver, Boulder, and Colorado Springs—typically feature open galleries, artist receptions, live music, and food trucks. First Friday Art Walks provide a great opportunity to explore local art scenes and support emerging artists without spending a dime on admission fees.

- **Outdoor Sculpture Gardens**: Visit a number of spectacular gardens, such as the Colorado Springs Fine Arts Center at Colorado College or the Benson Sculpture Garden in Loveland. These public art spaces showcase a diverse range of sculptures and installations in scenic outdoor settings, offering an enriching and low-cost artistic excursion.

Finding Local Nature Retreats & Hiking Groups

Maybe you find all this hiking exciting but don't think that you're quite ready to call Colorado home. But no matter where you live, chances are fairly decent that there are hiking opportunities within an hour of your house—and most people will find them even *closer* than that.

Find local hiking groups and see if you can use your love of the outdoors as a way of expanding your social circle.

La Isla Bonita: Retiring in the Caribbean

It might sound a little crazy at first, but retiring in the Caribbean is actually far more accessible than most people assume. The cost of living is very low and you'll enjoy access to an incredibly beautiful, almost dreamlike environment.

Below, we take a look at a few enticing Caribbean-based retirement opportunities.

Nassau, Bahamas: A Tropical Escape

The Bahamas are no doubt beautiful, but they're also paradise from a financial perspective. The islands have no income tax, wealth tax, sales tax, or inheritance tax. There is, however, an interesting clause to be aware of—and one that may make this retirement opportunity inaccessible for some.

To retire in Nassau, you need to become a permanent resident. To do that, you need to be able to purchase a property valued at least $750k.

Some retirees can accomplish this by selling their current home and maximizing the value of their retirement income through the island's tax benefits.

Those who *can* make it work benefit from beautiful beaches, luxurious spas, and access to several high-quality golf courses. Visit Paradise Island, snorkel along nearby reefs, and explore the vibrant downtown community. There's plenty to do.

Costa Rica: Pura Vida Lifestyle

Did you know that Costa Rica is referred to as a "Blue Zone" community? This means that people there consistently live longer than the average global lifespan. Costa Ricans can expect to live for about 80 years, almost three years longer than people living in the United States. So if you're looking to outlive some of your enemies, this just might be the place to do it.

Lower rates of obesity certainly contribute to this interesting statistic, but some experts think that there's a little more to it than that. Costa Ricans eat a rich varied diet, drink more vitamin-rich water, and generally report feeling a higher sense of purpose than Americans.

Costa Rica also has a comfortable climate, access to high-quality healthcare, and relatively affordable housing options. It's full of richly forested areas—including the Arenal Volcano National Park—and offers endless beach access, making it a practical and beautiful place to live out your retirement years.

Affordable Island Living in the Caribbean

Itching to live in this gorgeous region of the world? There are lots of ways to affordably make it happen. Naturally, the most desirable, resort-like destinations (think the Bahamas) tend to have the highest sticker price. In these communities, you'll need to be able to meet the high cost of housing, but you'll also most likely benefit from various tax incentives that make other aspects of personal finance more manageable.

If you'd like to retire in the Caribbean, start by considering what qualities your dream island needs to have. These can include everything from safety and culture to recreational activities. Once you've identified what you want, start researching how much it'll cost and go from there.

Finding Local Caribbean Culture Events & Groups

Interested in moving to the Caribbean but worried that you might experience too much of that social isolation we've been mentioning? While that's an understandable worry, rest assured that you won't be the only person there struggling to learn Spanish on Duolingo.

The Caribbean is a very common destination for American expats, and so there are lots of cultural and community groups where retirees like you can get together and mingle. As you get used to your new home, you'll also discover the great joy of getting to know the locals as well.

If you *do* happen to struggle with finding friends, look into community groups. If you're a spiritual person, you may find that church groups are a decent place to meet like-minded individuals. There will also be community centers and other social outlets not so different from the ones you're accustomed to in the United States.

Viva la Vida: Embracing Life in Mexico

Many people are a little nervous about the idea of retiring in Mexico. They know that the cost of living is low and that there's a plethora of natural beauty to enjoy. However, they're also very aware that parts of the country can be dangerous.

Is it safe or sensible to try and retire in Mexico? It certainly can be, as long as you take reasonable precautions and remain aware of your surroundings.

Latin America: Safer Than You Think (with These Tips)

Most Americans know that Chicago has a lot of violent crime. They also have no problem going there. Why? They do a little basic research, learn where to go and where to avoid, and while they're online, they look up a few great pizza joints to hit up while they're in town.

You can do the same with Mexico (although maybe swap out the pizza for delicious tacos). **Here's how to stay safe:**

- **Avoid Staying in "El Centro":** This name refers to basically the downtown area of any Latin American city. Like any downtown region, it'll often have higher rates of crime. If you don't know what you're doing, it's better to avoid the "El Centro" city sections after dark (and, sometimes, during the day depending on the city).

- **Learn Some Basics of the Language:** You know what's *not* super safe? Having no idea what anyone around you is saying. It helps enormously to be able to communicate on at least at a basic level with the people living in your community. We made a quip earlier about Duolingo, but it's actually a good idea. It'll help you enjoy a higher quality of life in terms of increased social opportunities, and it'll also be essential in any potential emergency. You can also take affordable one-on-one Spanish lessons with private tutors on a platform called iTalki.

- **Protect Your Phone:** It's never a great idea to walk around in a busy area with your face buried in your phone. For one thing, it tells any discerning criminal that you have something valuable to steal—and they might just walk or drive by and snatch it right out of your hands. It also indicates very clearly that you aren't paying attention to your surroundings. Don't make yourself a sitting duck.

With these basic precautions, you can enjoy a safe experience in Mexico and other Latin American countries. Below, we take a look at a few phenomenal locations that are worth checking out.

San Miguel de Allende: A Historic Treasure

Located in the Colonial Highlands region, San Miguel de Allende is noted for its mild climate and beautiful architecture. It has a very large population of foreigners—that would be you in this case—who make up 10% of all citizens. The cost of living is low, and it also has a big focus on the arts.

While there's a relatively high rate of petty crime, it's generally considered safe to live in and around the area. There's even a hot spring just 20 minutes outside of town.

Polanco, Mexico City: A Blend of Culture & Modernity

Polanco is actually a neighborhood in Mexico City—which happens to be the largest city in North America. For a major city, the cost of living is fairly low (less than *half* the cost of living in New York) and you still have access to all the metropolitan amenities. There's a wealth of greenery throughout the city too—much more than you may be used to in big American cities—with lush trees that line many blocks.

It's known for its art galleries and viewing opportunities, like the famous Soumaya museum. There are other intriguing museums a short drive away, like the Frida Kahlo museum in Coyoacan (the museum is actually her old house, and it's very colorful—she *was* a famed Mexican painter, after all!). Polanco is also within driving distance of the ancient city of Teotihuacan, and it has access to endless decadent restaurants. Be sure to check out the beautiful colony of Condesa as well, and taking a stroll through Parque Mexico is a priority.

Like any big city, there are dangerous parts of town to avoid (remember what we mentioned about "El Centro"), but if you like big city living without big city prices, it's unlikely that you'll find more bang for your buck—at least not in North America.

Puerto Vallarta: An Oceanside Paradise

Located near the ocean and flanked by the Sierra Madre mountain range, Puerto Vallarta is among the most scenic communities in North America. It features a vibrant culture and is known for its regular heritage festivals, old-fashioned Mexican architecture, and tempting street food.

While it *is* located in Jalisco—one of Mexico's more violent states with a notable cartel presence—Puerto Vallarta itself actually has a lower crime rate than most notable tourist communities, including Cabo and Cancun.

It also features a low cost of living, making it a great place to maximize the value of your retirement income.

Key Takeaways

- Relocating in retirement can be financially advantageous. Be on the hunt for great tax incentives—they're out there.

- When relocating, it may be smart to consider things that haven't previously been on your radar. For example, is there a large community of retirees? Does this community have adequate healthcare access?

- International relocation is often an affordable way to enjoy a higher quality of living at a significantly reduced cost.

- With a little bit of research and some proper precautions, you can safely live in many towns that often receive negative publicity in the news.

Chapter 8

Culinary Adventures for Foodies

"There is no sincerer love than the love of good food."

-George Bernard Shaw, playwright and critic

An excellent meal is always worth so much more than just the sum of its parts—particularly when you can share it with people you care about. Retirement is a great opportunity to explore the world of culinary delights—both as a chef and as someone with a big appetite. Below, we'll explore some of the most rewarding ways to experience the pleasures of food in your retirement years. Bring your stretchy pants!

Delicious Journeys Close to Home

We've mentioned a lot about traveling in this book, but you shouldn't have to go very far at all to find delicious food in your area. And sometimes, that food might come right from your own kitchen!

Cooking Up a Storm: Dinner Clubs

The phrase "dinner club" has different definitions depending on where you are and who you're talking to. There are very literal social organizations (similar to country clubs) that are labeled "dinner clubs," and while these tend to be a very upper-class environment, they *do* offer a great way to socialize over food.

You don't need country club money to eat with friends. You can start a dinner club with your friends or family, in which you take turns preparing each other's food or go to different restaurants within your community throughout the year.

They're a very nice way to stay social over some delectable food.

Finding Old School Farmers' Markets

Farmers' markets are an amazing way to find fresh produce and support local(ish) farmers in your community. They're actually enormously popular right now, both in rural and city environments.

Hot tip: Many state websites will have a farmers' market directory on their Department of Agriculture website, and you can use it to type in your location and find the market nearest you. (It might be the only reason anyone ever visits the Department of Agriculture's page, to be honest.)

Farmers' markets may sound quaint, but they're known for providing great prices on unique produce that you likely won't find at your big-box grocery store. Rainbow chard, anyone?

The Joy of Cooking Classes: Socializing While You Sizzle

Cooking classes can be a great way to learn niche skills. If you've ever wanted to learn how to make bread, sushi, or even your own cheese (remember when we intrigued you with this savory notion back in the first chapter?), chances are there's a class for that. You can definitely also find classes that cater to people in a more "I can't even make toast without burning it" category (no judgment).

They're a fun way to legitimately improve your skills in the kitchen and try recipes you might not have even heard of before. They also give you the chance to socialize with people who share a common interest with you.

You can find cooking classes all over the place—libraries, culinary schools, and even some restaurants offer them. Give it a Google. You'll be surprised by how many options are available in your community.

Dining at a Michelin-Starred Restaurant

Not everyone knows that the tire company Michelin cornered the market on fine dining recommendations a long time ago. While getting food recommendations from a car parts company might seem like it's in the same ballpark as getting your book recommendations from Home Depot, it's a well-established system that began in 1926.

Michelin's list is full of the type of places where the chef is a minor celebrity—or, in some cases, not so minor. Think Gordon Ramsay and his ilk.

Michelin-starred restaurants are well-known for being delicious—and almost always very expensive. But what's life anyway without the occasional splurge?

There are only about 200 Michelin-starred restaurants in the United States, so you'll likely need to do a little bit of travel to find one that interests you. Plan a trip around it! Just be sure to make your reservation well in advance, as these places fill up fast.

Budget-Friendly Luxury Dining Alternatives

Luxury dining is still achievable without booking a hotel room and waiting six months for a reservation. And, of course, everyone's definition of "luxury" is a little bit different. Italian restaurants are widely known for being a financially accessible option for luxury dining. You can get a really high-end pasta dish for around $30 a plate in most parts of the country, often while enjoying the dim lighting and attentive service that characterizes traditional fine-dining experiences.

There are also several notable luxury chains that you can find all over the country. Ruth's Chris is a well-known steakhouse that offers a relaxed but certainly highly luxurious dining experience. Its meals are very expensive—but ultimately more approachable than what you'll find at most of Michelin's favorite spots. There are plenty of similar luxury chains that, while pricey, offer a predictable yet slightly more approachable atmosphere for those new to luxury dining. Morton's, Capital Grille, McCormick and Schmick's, and many other chains will serve as a great introduction to highish-end dining.

Finding Local Food Festivals & Events

Local foodie festivals are a very affordable way to try lots of different kinds of foods. The fare that finds its way onto your fork will depend, of course, on the event's theme. An international food festival will give you the chance to try food from all over the world, while a chili cook-off might treat you to a much more familiar set of flavors.

If your community doesn't have a developed festival or event circuit, do a little digging—there are likely opportunities available within 50 miles of where you live. And hey, if you can't afford Michelin's picks, you can at least put their tires to good work in hopes of finding a decent meal.

Have Fork, Will Travel for Food

If you're planning on some retirement travel, you should think not just of locations you want to visit but also the food you'd like to try. While you can always import international flavors, it's never quite the same as experiencing them firsthand in the place where they originated.

Italy: Gelato, Pizza, Pasta & Truffle Hunting

Italy, as mentioned in a previous chapter, is very serious about fresh, local ingredients. If you embark on a tour of the country, you may be surprised to find the subtle ways that the menus change from location to location.

For instance, Rome is known for pizza and pasta. Bologna is where bologna meat sauce got its start. The Amalfi Coast has some of the best seafood dishes on the planet. Truffles you can find in many locations, though they have a particularly strong association with Umbria.

And while gelato got its start in Florence, you'll almost certainly find it everywhere.

American Food Festivals: BBQ, Lobsters, Chili & More

The US is *full* of food festivals, but most of them are highly localized. They don't usually generate national attention but instead quietly fill the hearts and stomachs of the people lucky enough to find them. That said, a few festivals do reach a more nationally known status. **Below are a number of well-known American food festivals to keep on your radar:**

- **The Big Apple Barbecue Block Party (New York City, New York):** A celebration of barbecue, featuring pitmasters from across the country showcasing their best smoked meats, sauces, and sides in Madison Square Park.

- **Maine Lobster Festival (Rockland, Maine):** A quintessential coastal festival celebrating Maine's famous lobster with delicious lobster dishes, cooking contests, and waterfront festivities.

- **Gilroy Garlic Festival (Gilroy, California):** A pungent celebration of all things garlic, featuring garlic-infused dishes, cooking competitions, and entertainment in the "Garlic Capital of the World." Bring breath mints.

- **International Chili Society World Championship Chili Cook-Off (various locations):** A fiery competition where chili chefs from around the world compete for the title of best chili, showcasing a variety of recipes and flavors.

While you're traveling for food, consider stopping by Terry Black's BBQ in Austin, Texas. It's a family-owned operation famous all over for its authentic and tasty barbeque, and it's truly a unique experience that you can't get anywhere else in the country.

Barbacoa Tacos in Mexico City

These feisty delights traditionally consist of shredded beef, lamb, or goat, which is cooked slowly in a delicious blend of spices and tasty broth. While you can find them anywhere, it's a particularly enticing treat to indulge in if you find yourself in Mexico City.

El Hidalguense, located in the Roma neighborhood, is well-known for its delicious barbacoa tacos. However, you'll likely find that there's no shortage of options.

In fact, every Saturday you'll see many "pop-up" barbacoa taco stands throughout the city streets, where you can sit down and have tacos for less than $1.50 each! Our personal favorite is on the corner of Avenida Veracruz and Parque España in the Condesa colony of Mexico City.

Sushi-Making Workshop in Japan

Sushi making is more accessible than many people first assume. It involves a relatively basic set of tools—a good knife and a sushi roller—as well as a little bit of patience. Seaweed and sushi rice can be purchased in most grocery stores, and from there it's a question of finding the ingredients that delight and excite you.

Because sushi traditionally consists of raw food, the quality of the ingredients is even more important than usual. You want vibrant, fresh flavors.

If you go to Japan, you may find that it's the perfect opportunity to sit in on a sushi-making workshop. There, you'll learn skills that'll make you a hit at every dinner party you attend.

Wine Tasting in Bordeaux, France

Bordeaux wine very naturally originates in the town of Bordeaux, France. Everyone has their own lyrical way of describing wine: "Fruity with a lingering taste of southern France sunlight" is a tantalizing if haute example. The actual sensory experience will depend largely on your pallet. Bordeaux wine typically tends to be dry with fruity, even citrusy notes but there are sweeter varieties available as well.

Even if you're the sort of person who thinks that all wine tastes like grape juice that was left out in the sun for too long, wine tasting in Bordeaux is a unique way to develop your palate while experiencing what the region is famous for.

Thai Cooking Course in Bangkok

Many American tastes aren't all that familiar with Thai cooking—and that is a certain shame. **Some well-known dishes include:**

- **Pad Thai:** A stir-fried noodle dish made with rice noodles, eggs, tofu or shrimp, bean sprouts, peanuts, and flavored with tamarind sauce, fish sauce, garlic, and chili.

- **Tom Yum Goong:** A hot and sour soup typically made with shrimp, mushrooms, lemongrass, kaffir lime leaves, galangal, lime juice, fish sauce, and chili peppers.

- **Green Curry (Gaeng Keow Wan):** A fragrant curry made with green curry paste, coconut milk, meat (usually chicken or beef), eggplant, Thai basil, and other vegetables.

- **Mango Sticky Rice (Khao Niew Mamuang):** A popular Thai dessert consisting of sweet sticky rice topped with ripe mango slices and drizzled with coconut milk.

- **Som Tum (Papaya Salad):** A refreshing and spicy salad made from shredded unripe papaya mixed with tomatoes, green beans, peanuts, lime juice, fish sauce, sugar, and chili peppers.

You'll surely work up a big appetite while exploring the temples and natural beauty of Thailand, so consider refueling at a cooking class or two. It's a great opportunity to learn how to make dishes that might not have ever occurred to you before. And if you struggle a bit, you can always eat the evidence.

Pastel de Nata in Portugal

This divine delight is a pastry that consists of a flaky crust and a sweet custard filling. While you don't have to travel to Portugal to find it, you'd be hard-pressed to find anywhere else with more diversity of options.

Fair warning: You'll likely eat more of it than you planned. But hey, there's no shame in wearing an elastic waistband on vacation. Besides, who are you going to run into that you know in Portugal?

Tapas in Seville, Spain

These mini yummies are basically Spanish appetizers. They can take many forms, some of which are very recognizable—like crostini or charcuterie—while others are a little more unique. Seville is particularly well-known for its vibrant Tapas culture.

You'll find them readily available in virtually every restaurant you visit. Be sure to diversify your choices a little bit to get the full experience. The best part? You'll be able to get a beer along with your tapas in most restaurants for as little as a buck or two!

Gyros in Greece

You just *can't* go to Greece and not get a gyro. At the most basic level, this delicious treat involves meat that's slow-cooked on a rotisserie and folded into a delicious pita. Lamb is used traditionally, but you'll find lots of variety.

Tripadvisor claims that the best gyros in Greece are being served up at Obelix restaurant in Fira on the island of Santorini. Whether or not they used a scientific method to reach that conclusion is hard to say. It'll be a spot worth checking out if you're in the area, but the truth is that you'll find no shortage of great options.

Pani Puri in India

This is a deliciously breaded and fried spherical dish that consists of chickpeas, potatoes, and onions. When visiting India, you'll see it everywhere—most often in carts providing quick street food. If you travel around the country, you'll notice slight variations in how the dish is prepared.

The Indian state of Madyah Pradhesh is known for serving pani puri with a creamier, almost mashed potato-like consistency in its center. In Maharashtra, on the other hand, it's commonly filled with chutney.

Variety is the spice of life, right?

Key Takeaways

- Splurging on the occasional gourmet meal can be a nice treat. Just remember that food doesn't need a Michelin star to be good. The luxury dining market is wide enough to suit many budgets.

- Cooking classes and demonstrations are an excellent way to learn new things and develop relationships with people in your community—all important ingredients for a healthy retirement.

- You don't have to travel the world to try new foods. Food festivals here in the US are a fun way to experience new flavors and learn more about other people's cultures.

- However, darting around the globe to try new foods is incredible! If you're planning to go abroad, do a little digging into the local flavors. It's very much worth the Google.

Chapter 9

The Smart Senior's Guide to Hobby Ideas

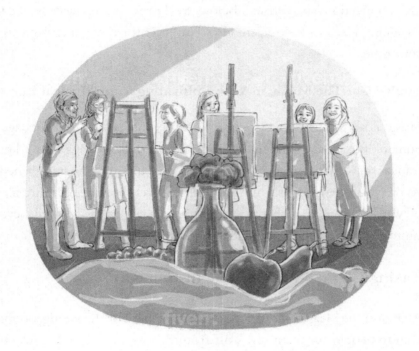

"Try new hobbies. Develop new interests. Pursue new experiences. When you expand your interests, you increase your opportunities for happiness."
-Richelle E. Goodrich, author

It's a simple concept: The more things that bring you joy, the easier it'll be to find happiness. We all know people who have started and stopped half a million hobbies or interests in their day. And maybe you're one of those people yourself (shhh…so are we).

While it's natural to feel a little bit embarrassed by the idea of flirting with a passion—knowing that you might talk it up to your friends and family only to one day drop it like a hot spud—know that there's no shame in it. New experiences are worth having, even when an instant love connection isn't formed. Below, we'll provide an overview of a few intriguing ideas to keep in mind as you look for rewarding ways to fill your time.

You've Got The Music in You: Cultivating Your Musical Ear

Music is an almost universal delight. Often hailed as "the language of humankind," it's a unifying art form that distills feelings into a lingua franca that virtually everyone can access and understand. Whether you're interested in it as a musician or just an enthusiast, there are plenty of ways to engage with this ancient art in ways that go well beyond simply having a carefully chosen Spotify playlist.

Taking Up the Violin (or Any Instrument)

Abandon the idea that learning an instrument is for the young. So many mature people cut themselves off from this source of joy because they think that it's something only kids have time for. Maybe they've even heard the statistic that learning an instrument becomes harder by the time you hit your twenties.

Here's the truth: If you're passionate and willing to work hard, you can learn *any* instrument. Maybe not to the extent that your local symphony will be beating down the door, but enough to add a little joy to your life.

You're likely to find that there are opportunities to rent instruments and enroll in lessons within your community. If you'd like to take baby steps, or maybe just save some money, there are also countless online resources. YouTube is a great place to get started, but there are also free or affordable apps that'll help you begin with the basics.

- **Yousician:** Provides interactive lessons and feedback for various instruments, including guitar, piano, ukulele, and bass, suitable for beginners and advanced players alike.

- **Simply Piano:** Uses gamified lessons and real-time feedback to teach piano, catering to all skill levels from beginner to advanced.

- **Fret Trainer:** Helps guitarists memorize the fretboard through interactive quizzes and exercises, enhancing fretboard fluency and improving playing ability.

Attending Classical Concerts, Symphonies & Chamber Music

Classical music is rewarding in that it not only provides you with a beautiful artistic experience to enjoy but it's also entrenched in rich history. Learn the terminology and the personal histories of the composers. Find local concerts and enjoy what writer Jean Paul Richter called "the poetry of the air."

Many people assume that classical music is the sole pleasure of the rich. While symphony tickets can be steep, there are many ways to enjoy it at an affordable price. Look for good deals on tickets, find out if any radio stations in your area broadcast live performances, and keep an eye peeled for free or low-cost events. Many symphonies have very active community outreach departments designed to make classical music more accessible.

Rocking Out at Local Clubs

You're never too old to head out to the club. True, you likely don't want to go out with the twenty-somethings of the world (honestly, who does?), but you'll most likely be surprised by how many venues cater directly to people in our age range.

You don't even have to go looking for 70s nights at your local bars—just find local acts or cover bands that you enjoy and start hitting up the shows in your area. You'll almost certainly find that most bands have fans consisting of people from many different age groups—including ours.

Taking a Closer Look at Live Jazz

Well-known jazz musician Herbie Hancock said that jazz is all about being in the moment. What better way to experience that than by physically attending live shows? Two of the many pleasures of jazz music is that no song is played exactly the same twice, and every artist puts their unique touch on the craft.

Research the live jazz opportunities available in your community—you may find that there are jazz bars within driving distance. And while traveling acts aren't nearly as prominent as they once were, you may also keep an eye out for incoming jazz musicians headed for a town near you.

Penny for Your Thoughts: Journaling & Writing

As mentioned in an earlier chapter, writing is a great way to help keep the mental cobwebs at bay. Not only does organizing your thoughts on the page sharpen your mind but it can also serve as a great way to unwind at the end of a long day.

Poet and playwright Oscar Wilde once said that he kept a diary so that he could have something scandalous to read later on. You can follow his example, or—if your life isn't quite as scandalous as his was—make the juicy parts up and enter fiction territory.

Benefits of Journaling for Mental Health

When you journal—even without writing the sort of things that would make Wilde blush—your brain experiences a gradual serotonin release. As you might recall, that's the chemical responsible for producing joy and relaxation.

Journaling also has more tangible mental health benefits. Many people find that it's easier to think clearly about the things that are bothering them when they can put their feelings down on the page.

It also strengthens your mental facilities. When you write in a journal, you're forcing yourself to think back and retrieve details from the past. With enough repetition, that can help strengthen your mind the same way daily crossword puzzles or regular reading can.

Creative Writing Workshops

Writer, journalist, and philosopher Christopher Hitchens, known for his sardonic wit, once suggested that everyone has a novel inside of them. He finished by saying, "which is exactly where it should remain." Well, who asked him?

Creative writing produces a similar response in your brain chemistry as journaling. You'll experience heightened relaxation and have a blast at the same time. You can certainly set out to do it on your own, but if you feel like a little guidance or structure would be helpful, there are plenty of ways to participate in writing workshops.

If you don't mind paying for it, your options are just about endless. See what courses are available online, or check in with your local community college. It'll almost certainly have creative writing workshops.

You should be able to find comparable free opportunities at your library or through any number of Facebook groups. You'll have to choke down a lot of clichéd advice ("show don't tell" and "adverbs pave the way to hell" and the like), but with enough determination, you might just develop some fairly skilled chops.

Self-Publishing Your Own Book or eBook

Writing a book is an *enormous* accomplishment. If you feel like sharing that achievement with your friends or family, there are plenty of ways to do it. Barnes and Noble offers a relatively low-cost printing service that'll allow you to produce attractive soft or hardback copies of your manuscript. This is a great option for people who want to distribute copies to their loved ones.

If you'd like to try your hand at selling to a wider audience, look into Amazon publishing. The platform makes it easy to publish print copies (it'll handle the printing for you), along with audio and digital versions of your book.

Don't know where to start? There are plenty of freelance editors available who can help you tighten your manuscript up.

Every Picture Tells a Story: Photography

You don't want to be that retired person who keeps posting blurry pictures of family dinners on Facebook. We all have pretty high-quality cameras in our pockets at virtually every moment, so wouldn't it be nice to learn how to use them?

There are endless opportunities to learn about photography in ways that go beyond the average smartphone. Below, we provide an overview of rewarding ways to engage with this art form.

Photography Tools & Gadgets You'll Love

Photography gadgets help enhance your existing camera or make it more adaptable for specific goals. For example, if you want to take a picture of yourself and some friends without asking for a stranger's assistance, you might use a selfie stick. If you want to do something slightly less annoying (our apologies, but those sticks *are* a bit silly looking), **you might use one of these tools:**

- **Smartphone Camera Lens Kit:** These kits offer additional lenses like fisheye, macro, and wide-angle that can be easily attached to your smartphone, allowing you to explore different perspectives and enhance your mobile photography.

- **GorillaPod Flexible Tripod:** This versatile tripod features bendable legs that can be wrapped around objects or adjusted on uneven surfaces, providing stability and creative freedom for capturing unique shots with your camera or smartphone.

- **Remote Shutter Release:** With a remote shutter release, you can trigger your camera remotely without physically touching it, helping to eliminate camera shake and ensuring sharp images, which is especially useful for long exposures or group shots.

- **Portable LED Light Panel:** Compact and adjustable LED light panels offer an easy way to improve lighting conditions for your photos or videos, particularly in low-light environments, allowing you to enhance the quality of your shots without carrying bulky equipment.

- **Photo Editing Software/App Subscription:** Subscribing to photo editing software or apps provides access to a wide range of editing tools and presets, empowering you to refine and enhance your photos' quality and creativity beyond just taking the shot. For example, Adobe Lightroom is a popular app for photo editing and helps you to make any photo look great.

Exploring Different Genres of Photography

It turns out that there are genres of photography that extend beyond merely "Instagram worthy." True photographers take a different approach to every subject that they shoot. **The following are a few photography genres you might want to keep in mind as you explore your new hobby:**

- **Macro:** Delves into the intricate details of small subjects like flowers, insects, or textures, revealing the hidden beauty and complexity often unnoticed by the naked eye.

- **Portrait:** Allows individuals or groups to be immortalized, revealing their unique personalities and emotions through careful lighting, posing, and composition.

- **Landscape:** Captures the expansive beauty of outdoor environments such as mountains, beaches, or forests, emphasizing composition and lighting to convey the majesty and tranquility of natural landscapes.

Photography Workshops & Tours

You'll likely find that there are many local resources for exploring photography. Your local library or community college may offer courses in which you can receive professional instruction. There are countless online resources from which you can learn proper techniques, or—if you're feeling brave—even have your photos critiqued by strangers online.

If you really become immersed in your hobby, you may even think about signing up for a photography tour. These are basically group trips organized around providing participants with the opportunity to capture the beauty of their subject matter on film.

For example, you might find photo tour opportunities centered around themes such as the Northern Lights, street art, wildlife. In short, if there's something that you're passionate about, chances are fairly decent that you can find an organization willing to charge you money to take pictures of it.

Your Life's Masterpieces: Painting & Drawing

It's been said that art doesn't have to be pretty to be meaningful. After all, it's all about the emotions you manage to distill on the canvas. You're never too old to pick up painting or drawing. Below, we highlight a few ways to get your creativity flowing.

Art Therapy: Getting Yer Yayas Out

Art therapy is all about processing your feelings in an environment that allows you to feel open and at peace. It can involve using paints, paper, pencils, or even clay. While it may sound a little "out there," it's a clinically proven approach to helping people deal with depression, anxiety, and other mental health struggles.

Professionals administering art therapy services will be licensed and have at least a master's degree.These services are more commonly available in city areas, but you may find local therapists in your community. If not, look for remote services online.

Attending Art Classes or Workshops

There are so many ways to enjoy art in a classroom environment. From the very relaxed "sips and splatters" style paint-by-numbers experience to the more structured opportunities you might find in a college setting, there's no shortage of opportunities.

- **Oil Painting Class:** Participants learn traditional techniques like color mixing and brushwork to create expressive artwork on canvas. These classes are commonly available at local art studios, community centers, universities, and online platforms such as Skillshare or Udemy.

- **Pottery Workshop:** These provide hands-on experience in crafting ceramic pieces, using techniques like handbuilding and wheel throwing.

- **Figure Drawing Session:** These are great opportunities to practice drawing the human form from live models, focusing on anatomy, proportion, and gesture. Sessions are often held at art schools, community colleges, and local art cooperatives, but you might also find them online.

Becoming a Gallery Docent

A docent is basically a volunteer tour guide at an art gallery or museum. While you can't exactly walk in off the street and start describing paintings to people—at least not in any museum-endorsed capacity— you can find and apply for opportunities in your community.

While it helps to have some background knowledge, you don't have to be an expert. Most museums will have a pre-screening interview and then a training process that'll help fill the gaps in your knowledge.

Laughter Is the Best Medicine

.... besides actual medicine, of course, but laughter actually *does* have medicinal value. It's been shown to reduce tension in the human body, accelerate recovery times, and alleviate the acute symptoms of stress, depression, and anxiety.

In other words, the more laughter you have in your life, the happier you'll ultimately be. Below, we provide a couple of mighty ways to get your jollies.

Side-Splitting Books by Hilarious Authors

Why not get your laugh on while you do your daily reading? **The following are a few writers whose books will make you laugh out loud:**

- **A Walk in the Woods by Bill Bryson:** A humorous and insightful memoir recounting Bryson's attempt to hike the Appalachian Trail, exploring both the beauty of nature and the challenges of long-distance hiking.

- **The Best of Me by David Sedaris:** A collection of essays by the acclaimed humorist, offering witty observations and personal anecdotes that range from the absurdities of everyday life to poignant reflections on family and identity.

- **Best. State. Ever. by Dave Barry:** A humorous travelogue by this Pulitzer Prize-winning author, chronicling his adventures and misadventures as he explores the quirks and charms of his home state of Florida.

Local Stand-Up Comedy & Open Mic Nights

Attending live comedy performances is a great way to share a laugh with your friends. Even if you don't have a comedy club in your area, you may find that many comedians will visit local concert venues, or, if they're big enough names, sports stadiums.

If you're very brave, you might even consider wandering up on stage to try your hand at an open mic night. Just be sure to spend some time punching up those jokes during your daily writing sessions. No one wants to bomb on stage (although it *will* be comedy for the audience— your call!).

Earning Money with Hobbies You Love

While hobbies are better known for *costing* money rather than earning it, there are plenty of ways to pick up a little extra side cash by doing things you like. The kids today call it a "side hustle." Let's examine just a few of the many ways to cash in on your interests.

School Sports: Part-Time Coaching

You definitely don't become rich by coaching school sports. Most coaches earn minimum wage, and many others are just volunteers.

But even if the cash isn't great, there are other benefits that should be on your radar. Throughout this book, we've emphasized the benefits of mentorship, but coaching a sports team will also keep you physically active. Blowing that whistle has to burn *some* calories, right?

Crafts: Starting Your Own Etsy Store

Etsy is an innovative way to sell your art online. It doesn't even have to be limited to paintings, drawings, or sculptures—you can sell knitted items, graphic design services, and even homemade costumes. The sky, as they say, is the limit.

Driving for Dollars: Food Deliveries & Rideshares

While grocery shopping likely isn't a hobby of yours—we should hope not after reading a book about 150 things to do in retirement—it *is* a relatively relaxed way to earn a few extra dollars by shopping for someone else. You can get out of the house, fire up a podcast, and spend as little or as much time as you'd like getting paid for something you usually do for yourself for free. No one's yet come up with a way for you to get paid for shopping for your *own* groceries, unfortunately, but there's always hope!

Selling Your Handiwork: Sewing, Knitting & Crocheting

Sewing is quickly going by the wayside as a skill. If you have a knack for needles, you'll likely find that there are lots of people in your community—or online—who are willing to pay for your crafty quirks. Advertise on Facebook groups and other community forums like Nextdoor, or open up one of those Etsy stores mentioned earlier.

More Side Hustle Ideas for Retirees

It's easier than ever to earn some extra income. If you do become quite skilled at writing, you'll find plenty of freelancing opportunities on platforms like Upwork or Fiverr. There are similar opportunities available for editors, graphic designers, or even musicians and photographers.

Side hustles are a great way to stay busy and supplement your retirement income. You have to pay for that culinary trip to the Amalfi Coast we mentioned earlier somehow!

Key Takeaways

- Creative hobbies are a great way to stay active while nurturing your mental health.

- Even if there aren't many creative outlets within your community, you'll find no shortage of opportunities online.

- Hobbies and interests can have revenue potential. Look for ways that you can earn money doing the things that put a smile on your face.

Chapter 10

Leaving Your Comfort Zone: Thrills for the Bold

> "If you want to achieve your goals, you must be willing to step out of your comfort zone."
> **- Germany Kent, author and journalist**

The "life begins at the end of your comfort zone" mantra has been recycled and repackaged in a million different phrases and slogans. It's definitely a cliché, but one that's been at the heart of the human experience since the beginning of time. It's what virtually every good story that's ever been told is about.

In this chapter, we'll explore some of the pleasures available to people who are willing to leave the familiar behind in favor of something bold and exciting.

All the World's a Stage: Acting & Theater Writing

Acting and theater writing are more accessible than you think. If you're reading this with skepticism and a scoff, ask yourself this: Does your community have a local theater group? An acting troupe or even a sketch comedy club?If so, they'll almost certainly be actively looking for new participants all the time. If you aren't ready to step on stage, they'll be all too glad to accept your help with set building, ticket taking, or even operating the lights. You'll almost certainly not be paid for this, but it's your foot into the theatrical door!

Your local community college may have acting or even playwriting classes, and there are also online resources. As mentioned earlier, YouTube is a fantastic place to learn basically anything for free. MasterClass is a more formal online learning platform in which writers, actors, and many other types of celebrities offer paid classes, supplying you with the tricks of their trade.

In other words, there are *many* ways to get into the performing arts, regardless of your age or background.

Below are a few suggestions for getting started:

Intro to Acting: Discovering Your Inner Thespian

Introductory acting classes will generally provide you with a mixture of theory and practice. You'll learn techniques that actors have been applying on the stage and screen for generations, and then you'll usually have the chance to give them a whirl yourself.

The online resources mentioned above are a great way to dip your toes in the water, but it's better to get yourself into a group environment if you can. Acting is a very dynamic experience, and it helps enormously if you can draw inspiration from what's happening in the room—even if that thing is a twenty-something-year-old stammering through Shakespeare's monologues.

Finally Writing Your Stageplay or Screenplay

If you're interested in creative writing but find the idea of writing an 80kword novel a little daunting, a screenplay or stageplay could be a happy middle ground. These usually clock in at around 20k words or less, and they let you focus less on the technical aspects of writing and more on putting together exciting scenes and vivid characters.

You'll find screenwriting resources in many of the same places where you'll encounter other creative instruction—colleges, libraries, and online groups.

One thing to keep on your radar: Screenplay and stageplay formatting is very particular. If you ever decide that you want to do more with your manuscript than simply hide it in a drawer, you'll need to get those details right.

Many popular screenplay writing tools like Final Draft (which is used by almost 100% of professional productions) automate most of these requirements, making it worth your consideration.

Improvisation: Thinking on Your Feet

You likely thought that you were done embarrassing your kids after they grew up and left the house, but here comes improv to mortify them all over again. Improvisation involves little more than a few brave people getting on a stage and simply seeing what happens. Audience members supply the group with the setting, the characters, and the scenario, and it goes from there. Where? Nobody knows! That's the beauty of improv.

Much of the time, the performers wind up having more fun than anyone in the audience. And every once in a while, you'll come across a group that *really* nails it. The important thing is just to have fun.

An improv group will supply you with a nice social outlet and (hopefully) provide you with a regular dose of that medicinal laughter mentioned in the previous chapter.

Many cities will have multiple options to choose from. While it's fair to say that you likely won't walk right through the door and make your way into their traveling group, you'll probably find that they offer workshops. Even really well-known groups like Second City offer classes.

Script Writing & Directing: Getting Behind the Scenes

Producing a screenplay or stageplay is a big project, but there are ways to do it on a tight (or even non-existent) budget. If you believe that your manuscript is ready to be experienced by the wider world, start by thinking very practically about whether the content is easily adaptable for the stage.

Are there any explosions or ten-story monsters in it? That'll likely need a rewrite. Are you holding out hope that your script may work its way up the ladder? Maybe land a big star like Julia Roberts for the lead? Good luck—we hear that she's busy.

Also, traditional channels are slow moving and it could take a year or more before you even hear back from any agents or production houses.

An easier path may be to start locally. Are there any community theater groups that might be willing to produce your stageplay and maybe let you be involved in it? Can you feasibly put the production on yourself? People do it, and often for less money than you might at first assume.

If you're interested in going the indie stage/film route, do some research first. It's not impossible, but it'll require some careful planning. Chat with a local theater director to find out what kind of a budget is needed to rent a venue and put a set together.

Adventure Sports: Take a Walk on the Wild Side

We did mention at the beginning of the chapter that adventure awaits you. Adventure sports provide a very real mental health benefit that psychologists refer to as "hedonic well-being." In less-fancy English, that means immediate and consuming joy. When you're involved in an activity that feels thrilling and maybe a little dangerous, it virtually eliminates any chance of past or future orientation. You're living only in the moment.

Some people meditate to improve their mindfulness, while others choose to jump out of a plane. We support both choices.

Skydiving: The Ultimate Adrenaline Rush

Did you know that only 0.0011% of skydiving expeditions result in fatalities [21]? Granted, most recreational activities don't even beg the question, "How many people die doing this?", but it *is* a reassuring statistic.

Skydiving has been shown to produce long-term mental health benefits in terms of improved stress management. Once your brain has experienced the fear of freefalling from thousands of feet in the sky, it's ready for just about anything.

Whitewater Rafting: Riding the Rapids

We teased you with this in the Introduction to this book, but we weren't kidding. Whitewater rafting is a fast-paced way to explore rivers and nature in general. Participants hop on a (usually inflatable) raft and set out for the ensuing adventure. The "white" aspect refers to the way the water looks when it's moving quickly—and it *will* move quickly.

You'll find short excursions that last for several hours or longer opportunities that can last for days and involve camping out on riverbanks.

Naturally, you'll require access to a fast-moving body of water. This may mean traveling a little bit, but it's worth the gas mileage as there are some incredible trips to be had from it. Explore the Alaskan wilderness. Venture through canyons in Utah. Tackle the mountain ranges in Colorado. There are countless unforgettable ways to get your whitewater rafting fix.

The best news? You don't need any prior training to get started. Most whitewater rafting services will allow you to rent equipment from them, and they'll also provide guides to ensure safety and accessibility.

Reach New Heights with Mountain & Rock Climbing

As with anything else, mountain and rock climbing are what you make of them. You can start at a climbing wall at your local YMCA and then graduate to a much larger mountain range. And you're never too old to get started—Japanese skier and alpinist Yuichira Miura climbed Mount Everest at age 70!

Climbing is great exercise, working most of your major muscle groups and allowing you to burn around 900 calories an hour.

However, it's a wise idea to start slow. Take a rock-climbing class at a local indoor venue where the conditions are safe and controlled, and then ascend to new heights from there.

Finding Local Adventure Sports Facilities & Clubs

Your ability to find local adventure sports clubs may depend largely on your geographical proximity to adventure sports locations. If you're close to a mountain or a river, your options will be abundant. Otherwise, you might need to get a bit creative.

If nothing else, you might find indoor rock-climbing venues, hiking groups, biking clubs, or other groups that focus on getting outdoors and having some fun.

If you can't find anything near you, hop online. There are so many Facebook groups out there that are dedicated to adventure sports. You're bound to find a passionate community ready to offer practical tips for people getting started at any age.

Pursuing Personal Passions

What gets your heart racing? Let's be honest here: The daily grind doesn't involve or even *support* the conditions required for our passions to flourish. In retirement, you have all the time in the world to change that. But first, you need a clear idea of what that means for you.

In many ways, that's what this book has been all about—thinking outside the box to find activities that light your pants on fire (but hopefully not literally). We tell kids to follow their dreams all the time, but are we brave enough to do it ourselves?

We like to think so. Below are a few suggestions for getting started.

Transforming Your Childhood Dreams Into Adult Adventures

When we're kids, we want so many things—but we usually have to settle for what we're given. As an adult, it's the opposite. Everything we have is the product of our efforts, but we're often so busy that we don't have time to think deeply about what we want.

If you're looking for inspiration, think about what you dreamed of doing as a child. Maybe that means trying your hand at writing, acting, or performing, as mentioned earlier.

Maybe it means taking up a new hobby. Did you want to own a pony? That's a cliché we can work with. Give horseback riding a try. Did you want to be a brave knight? Explore archery or fencing. Did you love fantasy and adventure? Find out what it would take to go on a European castle tour.

Many childhood dreams are at the very least inspired by *real* possibilities, so see if you can do something kind for your inner kid.

Starting a Blog or Podcast: Share Your Voice

Blogging and podcasting are affordable ways to share your voice and potentially even develop an audience. The startup cost for blogging is nearly non-existent—sites like WordPress offer plug-and-play templates that allow you to start publishing online content with no web design skills required.

Podcasting will require a little more background knowledge. You'll need to learn a bit about audio editing and recording basics, but remember that there are always resources out there to help. Any question that comes up has an answer that's, in this technological age, only a click or two away. The easiest way to do it is to record the audio on Audacity (a free recording software that's easily downloadable), run it through Adobe Podcast (a cheap AI editing software that cleans up the audio), and upload it to Buzzsprout (a podcast hosting platform that automatically uploads your podcast to Spotify, Apple, and other common podcast platforms). And voila—you could have an audience of millions waiting for you (or maybe hundreds, but this isn't a popularity contest).

Learning a New Language: Unlock New Cultures

Learning a foreign tongue is a great way to immerse yourself in a different culture. It's also very handy if you plan on doing any of the international travel recommended earlier in the book. It'll definitely take some work and persistence, but you may be surprised by how quickly you'll progress once you get started.

You can always buy translation dictionaries and tapes, but don't sleep on the incredibly helpful and convenient digital resources available. As the old Apple commercial said, there's an app for that.

Before are a few that we like:

- **iTalki:** The best way to learn a language is by having conversations with native speakers. iTalki connects you with teachers around the globe and makes it easy to have one-on-one language learning lessons, often for less than $10 per hour!

- **Rosetta Stone**: Renowned for its immersive teaching method, Rosetta Stone offers interactive lessons focusing on speaking, listening, reading, and writing skills. Its emphasis on context and real-life situations helps learners grasp language naturally.

- **Babbel**: This platform provides comprehensive lessons designed by linguistic experts. It offers courses tailored to your native language, making it easier to understand and learn. With a focus on practical vocabulary and grammar, Babbel helps learners quickly build conversational skills.

- **Duolingo**: With its gamified approach, Duolingo makes language learning fun and engaging. It offers bite-sized lessons covering reading, writing, listening, and speaking. The app tracks your progress and adapts difficulty levels to individual learning styles, making it suitable for learners of all levels.

Public Speaking: Conquer Your Fears

Did you know that, statistically, people are more afraid of public speaking than they are of death? That begs an old Seinfeld joke: "At a funeral, most people would rather be in the coffin than giving the eulogy."

That's likely not entirely true, but it *does* reflect the fact that getting in front of an audience is a major source of discomfort for many people.

Here are two things to consider: First, public speaking is associated with producing an anti-aging effect on your brain. When you learn new skills and push boundaries, it strengthens your mind. And second, it also helps you process stress and anxiety. The more you face your fears, the better your brain becomes at managing them.

Acting classes and theater experiences are natural ways to get public speaking opportunities. You can even take public speaking classes at most community colleges.

Heart of Gold: Embracing Philanthropy in Retirement

We mentioned earlier that many retirees enjoy contributing to causes that they're passionate about more than travel—or virtually any other leisure activity for that matter. Not only do charitable causes fill your schedule but they also create a sense of purpose and nurture social connections.

Below, we'll look at how you can pick and support a cause that you care about.

Finding Your Passion: How to Choose a Cause

Finding an organization, charity, or relief effort to support is as simple as thinking about what moves you the most. If you're passionate about helping children thrive, there are a million organizations that fight food insecurity or work on mentoring initiatives. Big Brothers and Big Sisters are great examples, but there are many others.

If you're passionate about the arts, try organizations that make cultural events more accessible to low-income families. For example, the National Endowment for the Arts might be a fantastic way to channel your inner do-gooder.

Maybe there are so many worthy causes that you just can't pick. Try perusing a website called "The Life You Can Safe." This is a charitable organization itself, built around identifying high-impact causes that, very literally, save lives.

Realistic Budgeting for Charitable Giving

The amount of money you decide to donate to charity is ultimately a very personal choice. Some people structure their entire lives around charitable giving, while others donate only when they're overcome by social pressure at the grocery store checkout line.

If you're serious about making regular charitable contributions, it helps to look at it practically. Naturally, the money will need to come out of the "discretionary" category of your budget.

Decide for yourself how much you can give. Are you willing to modify your lifestyle to give more, or would you prefer to help out in ways that don't significantly impact your finances?

Both perspectives are completely valid. As you explore charitable giving, do a little research on what that looks like from a tax standpoint. You can usually deduct up to 60% of your income (though most people don't donate nearly that much), but some organizations have a lower deduction ceiling.

Making a Difference: Starting Your Own Nonprofit

If you're fully committed to making a difference but have found that no existing organization is quite making the change you'd like to see in the world, it may be time to start your own non-profit. That said, it won't be easy. There are many legal requirements that need to be satisfied, and plenty of fundraising that'll have to be done.

It's a good idea to get your feet wet with an established organization so that you can learn the ropes in a lower-stakes environment. There are also online legal resources like LegalZoom and Rocket Lawyer that may help you satisfy state and federal requirements at a lower cost than you'd experience hiring a traditional attorney.

Key Takeaways

- Adventure isn't just fun—it also stimulates and strengthens the mind, potentially reducing cognitive aging.

- Facing your fears is also medicinal. Engaging healthily with your stressors trains your brain to become better at handling anxiety.

- Your community likely has plenty of ways for you to step out of your comfort zone. Try acting, writing, or improv groups—your creativity is just waiting to be unleashed.

- Charity is an excellent way to add joy to your life. Find a cause you care about or start your own.

Final Thoughts

If this book has taught you anything, it should be that there are endless ways to follow your bliss. There's no such thing as a retirement manual because everyone is ultimately going to gravitate to different things. **But here's what's true for _all_ of us:**

- An enjoyable retirement is accessible with almost any budget. You don't need a seven-figure brokerage account—you just need to be able to look for sources of joy that fit within your means.

- Travel is a great pleasure, but there's no single way to do it. Some people are jet setters in retirement, while others prefer staying closer to home. Both approaches have their rewards.

- Hobbies and interests are part of a healthy retirement lifestyle. Activities that stimulate your mind and force you to interact with other people improve your mental and emotional health. Look for regular opportunities to put your mind to work.

- Exercise is important, but it doesn't necessarily require joining a gym. The key is to find sustainable physical activities. Bike riding, swimming, and hiking are great ways to stay in shape, and they're also easy on your joints.

- You're never too old to follow your dreams, so look for activities that excite and delight you. And if that means stepping out of your comfort zone, all the better. Write that story. Tell that joke. Get up on a stage and perform. Life is at its best when we're finding new joys to stir our spirits and keep us young at heart.

Key Takeaways

We explored an incredible number of suggestions in this book—all of which ran the gamut in terms of varying price points. Traveling the world may be enjoyable, and it certainly *is* a retirement cliché, but keep in mind that it's just one of the many ways to enjoy your new lifestyle.

Remember what we mentioned earlier: Many retired people *aren't* jet setting. They aren't spending a ransom of money on anything in particular. In fact, studies show that the happiest retirees have developed a routine that provides them with a regular supply of healthy stimulation. This means human interactions. Reading, writing, and deep thought. Exercise. But most importantly? A sense of purpose. You need to look for things that you're *passionate* about. Volunteer at a food bank. Look into becoming a docent at a nearby museum. Find something that gets you excited to leave the house, and pursue it with all the energy you're willing to spare.

As you plan out your retirement schedule, think about how much time you're trying to fill. Very likely, you used to work for 40 or more hours a week. While you might not want to take your retirement activities that far, around half of that time commitment could be a decent starting point. But keep in mind that finding just twenty hours worth of things to do in a week can be hard if you're not actively working at it, so discover your passions and pursue them with vigor.

While there may be a momentary post-employment slump in which you find yourself feeling a little depressed (or at the very least a little bit off), try your best to stay the course. If those feelings are being caused by your significant life change, they'll almost certainly dissipate as you build a new routine that *you* find meaningful.

There are so many ways to enjoy your sunset years. None of them are inherently better than the others. Now is the time to follow your bliss— whatever that might be and however it might look.

Retirement is certainly not the end. It's the beginning of a whole new adventure. Now that you have the tools, it's time to go out and use them.

We'll see you on the sunny shores of Costa Rica. Or on the green of the golf course. Or onstage at improv. With all the options we've listed within this book, we're bound to run into one another somewhere!

A Parting Gift

As a way of saying thank you for your purchase, we're offering two FREE downloads that are exclusive to our book readers!

First, the **Retirement Movie Marathon PDF**. We've handpicked 27 feel-good films that are more than just flicks—they're gateways to laughter, inspiration, and heartwarming journeys. From laugh-out-loud comedies to soul-stirring romances, each movie is a toast to the joys and adventures of retirement.

Second, the **Adventure Checklist: 20 Outdoor Activities for Retirees**! This is your all-access pass to excitement, exploration, and the sheer joy of the great outdoors. Whether you're looking to reconnect with nature, pump up the adrenaline, or simply try something new and delightful, we've handpicked 20 activities to add zest to your days.

To download your bonuses, go to monroemethod.com/retirement-fun or simply scan the QR code below (just use the camera app on your smartphone!).

Can You Do Us a Favor?

Thanks for checking out our book.

We're confident that it'll help you have an action-packed and fun retirement!

Might you take 60 seconds and write a quick blurb about this book on Amazon?

Reviews are the best way for independent authors (like us) to get noticed, sell more books, and spread our message to as many people as possible. We also read every review and use the feedback to write future revisions—and also future books.

Just navigate to the link below or scan the QR code to leave your review!

mybook.to/retirement-fun

Thank you—we really appreciate your support.

About the Author

Garrett Monroe is a pen name for a team of writers with expertise in business, retirement planning, and estate planning. A few writers on the team have already retired themselves, and have come together to share their knowledge and produce a series of retirement books to help you have an amazing, fulfilling, and abundant retirement.

References

1. Gardner B, Lally P, Wardle J. Making health habitual: the psychology of 'habit-formation' and general practice. Br J Gen Pract. 2012 Dec;62(605):664-6. doi: 10.3399/bjgp12X659466. PMID: 23211256; PMCID: PMC3 505409.

2. Dang L, Ananthasubramaniam A, Mezuk B. Spotlight on the Challenges of Depression following Retirement and Opportunities for Interventions. Clin Interv Aging. 2022 Jul 7;17:1037-1056. doi: 10.2147/CIA.S336301. PMID: 35855744; PMCID: PMC9288177.

3. Patel, R. (2023, November 16). *A practical guide to setting clear financial goals: Why it matters.* Medium. https://rprahuldpatel.medium.com/a-practical-guide-to-setting-clear-financial-goals-why-it-matters-73cb1423ecfb

4. Nidirect. (2023, January 6). *Staying mentally active.* Nidirect. https://www.nidirect.gov.uk/articles/staying-mentally-active#:~:text=Physical%20activity-,Mental%20stimulation,easier%20you'll%20find%20remembering.

5. Zaidel DW. Art and brain: insights from neuropsychology, biology and evolution. J Anat. 2010 Feb;216(2):177-83. doi: 10.1111/j.1469-7580.2009.01099.x. Epub 2009 May 28. PMID: 19490399; PMCID: PMC2815940.

6. *5 Ways Mother Nature Can Lift Your Mood | Premier Health.* (n.d.). Premier Health. https://www.premierhealth.com/your-

health/articles/women-wisdom-wellness-/5-Ways-Mother-Nature-Can-Lift-Your-Mood/#:~:text=Breathing%20fresh%20air%20can%20raise,increases%20the%20production%20of%20endorphins.

7. Greeson JM, Chin GR. Mindfulness and physical disease: a concise review. Curr Opin Psychol. 2019 Aug;28:204-210. doi: 10.1016/j.copsyc.2018.12.014. Epub 2018 Dec 27. PMID: 30785067; PMCID: PMC6597336.

8. *Step counting | The fact and fiction of walking 10,000 steps a day.* (n.d.). https://www.nuffieldhealth.com/article/walking-10k-steps-a-day-fact-fiction#:~:text=The%20idea%20of%20walking%2010%2C000,and%20the%20idea%20caught%20on.

9. *9 Benefits of yoga.* (2021, August 8). Johns Hopkins Medicine. https://www.hopkinsmedicine.org/health/wellness-and-prevention/9-benefits-of-yoga

10. *U.S. Bicycle Route System - Adventure Cycling Association.* (2024, February 26). Adventure Cycling Association. https://www.adventurecycling.org/routes-and-maps/us-bicycle-route-system/#:~:text=Over%2018%2C000%20miles%20are%20currently,and%20many%20routes%20are%20signed.

11. Cscs, G. B. M. C. C. (2023, August 7). *Is There Such thing as "Too Young" for a Heart Attack? | Louisville KY | UofL Health.* UofL Health | Louisville Hospital and Health Care System Serving Kentucky and Indiana. https://uoflhealth.org/articles/is-there-such-thing-as-too-young-for-a-heart-attack/

12. Nakamura et al. Stress Repression in Restrained Rats by (R)-(-)-Linalool Inhalation and Gene Expression Profiling of Their Whole Blood Cells. *Journal of Agricultural and Food Chemistry*, 2009; 57 (12): 5480 DOI: 10.1021/jf900420g

13. Pew Research Center. (2023, February 2). *Key findings about online dating in the U.S. | Pew Research Center.* https://www.pewresearch.org/short-reads/2023/02/02/key-findings-about-online-dating-in-the-u-s/#:~:text=About%20half%20of%20those%20under,of%20those%2065%20and%20older.

14. Boudreau P, Mackenzie SH, Hodge K. Adventure-based mindsets helped maintain psychological well-being during COVID-19. Psychol Sport Exerc. 2022 Sep;62:102245. doi: 10.1016/j.psychsport.2022.102245. Epub 2022 Jun 17. PMID: 35755019; PMCID: PMC9212858.

15. Spirovski, M. (2022, September 22). *15 Interesting Nonprofit Organizations Statistics and Facts.* TeamStage. https://teamstage.io/nonprofit-organizations-statistics/#:~:text=billions%20in%20revenue.-,How%20many%20nonprofits%20are%20in%20the%20US%20in%202022%3F,charities%2C%20and%20other%20nonprofit%20organizations.

16. *How many countries in Africa? - Worldometer.* (n.d.). https://www.worldometers.info/geography/how-many-countries-in-africa/#:~:text=There%20are%2054%20countries%20in,the%20United%20Nations%20official%20statistics).

17. Author, N. (2022, April 14). *Buddhists | Pew Research Center.* Pew Research Center's Religion & Public Life Project. https://www.pewresearch.org/religion/2012/12/18/global-religious-landscape-buddhist/#:~:text=Seven%20countries%20have%20Buddhist%20majorities,Sri%20Lanka%2C%20Laos%20and%20Mongolia.

18. Waldek, S. (2024, January 11). The best time to book a flight for domestic, international, and summer travel. *Travel + Leisure.* https://www.travelandleisure.com/travel-tips/when-to-book-flights-for-cheapest-airfare

19. Zhekova, D. (2023, December 22). This midwestern city is the most affordable place to retire in the U.S., according to a new report. *Travel + Leisure.* https://www.travelandleisure.com/toledo-ohio-is-the-most-affordable-us-city-to-retire-8418755#:~:text=It%20found%20that%20living%20in,in%20a%20thriving%20retiree%20community.

20. Barthel C, Halvachizadeh S, Gamble JG, Pape HC, Rauer T. Recreational Skydiving-Really That Dangerous? A Systematic Review. Int J Environ Res Public Health. 2023 Jan 10;20(2):1254. doi: 10.3390/ijerph20021254. PMID: 36674008; PMCID: PMC9859333.

Made in United States
Orlando, FL
09 November 2024

53479993R00108